FLAvv ED
&
Fabulous

FLAWED
&
Fabulous

A Memoir of a Working
Mother's Pursuit
of ~~Happiness~~
Wholeness

SHARI CHELACK

This book is a work of memoir. It reflects the author's present recollections of experiences over time. The author has tried to recreate events, locales and conversations to the best of her ability from her memories of them. Nonetheless, some of the names and personal or identifying characteristics of the individuals, physical properties, occupations, and places of residence involved have been changed in order to disguise and protect the privacy of their identities.

Although the author and publisher have made every effort to ensure that the information in this book was correct at press time, the author and publisher do not assume and hereby disclaim any liability to any party for any loss, damage, or disruption caused by errors or omissions, whether such errors or omissions result from negligence, accident, or any other cause.

The author of this book does not dispense medical advice or prescribe the use of any technique as a form of treatment for physical, emotional, or medical problems without the advice of a physician or therapist, either directly or indirectly. This book is not intended as a substitute for medical advice of physicians or therapists. The intent of the author is only to offer information of a general nature to help you in your quest for emotional and spiritual well-being. In the event you use any of the information in this book for yourself, which is your constitutional right, the author and the publisher assume no responsibility for your actions.

ISBN (Paperback Edition): 978-1-989840-12-2
ISBN (eBook Edition): 978-1-989840-13-9

Cover Design by Fiona Jayde Media, www.fionajaydemedia.com
Edited by Talena Winters, www.mysecretwishpublishing.com
Interior Design by The Deliberate Page, www.deliberatepage.com
Author Photo © Gentil Photography, www.gentilphotography.com. Used by Permission.

Printed in the United States of America, or the country of purchase.

First Printing Edition: September 2020

Grateful acknowledgment is made to the following for permission to reprint previously published material:

Penguin Random House: Excerpt taken from *Rising Strong* by Brené Brown Copyright © 2015 by Brené Brown. Used by permission of Penguin Random House. www.penguinrandomhouse.com

Penguin Random House: Excerpt taken from *Wild* by Cheryl Strayed Copyright © 2012 by Cheryl Strayed. Used by permission of Penguin Random House. www.penguinrandomhouse.com

TED: Excerpt taken from Sir Ken Robinson, *Do Schools Kill Creativity?* TED2006. To watch the full talk, visit www.TED.com

Thomas Nelson: Excerpt taken from *Girl, Wash Your Face: Stop Believing the Lies About Who You Are So You Can Become Who You Were Meant to Be* by Rachel Hollis Copyright © 2018 by Rachel Hollis. Used by permission of Thomas Nelson. www.thomasnelson.com

Zondervan: Excerpt taken from *Present over Perfect* by Shauna Niequist Copyright © 2016 by Shauna Niequist. Used by permission of Zondervan. www.zondervan.com

To my parents, for providing me a childhood every child deserves;

To my husband, for loving me through it all; and

To my children, for waking me up and completing my story.

"But once I had brains, and a heart also; so, having tried them both, I should much rather have a heart."

~ L. Frank Baum, *The Wonderful Wizard of Oz*, c. 1900 ~[*]

Contents

Not in Kansas Anymore

The early years of raising babies are supposed to be a magical, fairy-tale experience, right?

Well, that wasn't the case for me. I would have loved to have stumbled upon a how-to parenting manual to guide me through those primary years. As a new mom, I searched for the enchantment everyone spoke of, but I couldn't see past the chaos engulfing me. Where was the pixie dust? Why was I constantly drowning beneath heaps of dirty dishes and forever cleaning grimy handprints off the walls?

I was in a constant mode of cringing, grinding my teeth, and fighting for breath under the crashing waves of life. It probably didn't help that I held the equivalent of a full-time job, juggling a corporate career during the week, while assisting my husband in running our trucking business during the weekend hours. The remainder of my weekends were spent cleaning, making food, and preparing for the demanding week ahead. There was no time for pleasure or amusement in trying to do everything.

I look back and remember one instance when I found myself isolated with my two baby boys in the underwear aisle of Walmart. Resigned at last to my new mommy rear-end—carefully constructed through a combination of having two children under three and no energy to work out—I was finally purchasing underwear that fit (and couldn't care less if anyone noticed they looked made for a small beluga whale).

A starry-eyed, middle-aged women approached, coming too close for comfort. She gazed at my three-year-old, Bentley, who was belted into the child seat. Behind him was a small mountain composed of our groceries for the week, a diaper bag, and the baby carrier containing my six-month-old, Weston. The woman leaned in and gushed, "*These* are the days, aren't they? Cherish them while your babies are young. I often wish I was in your stage of life again."

I stared at her, my mouth agape.

Are you kidding, lady, these are the days?

I wasn't fit for public viewing—my naked face revealed the dark circles under my eyes and my hair had not been washed in days. I was wearing leggings I hadn't needed until my sixth month of pregnancy with my first child, but which were now the most comfortable and best-fitting item I owned. I was exasperated, running on caffeine and too little sleep. I was wearing a Depends pad, just in case I peed myself (thank you, Baby Number One) and was purchasing oversized underwear from Walmart, for goodness' sake.

A random blast of air reminded me my baby, Weston, needed to be changed, and his fussiness told me we were approaching his feeding time. I would have to find a random spot in Walmart and set up camp—always a pleasant experience.

But my unwanted guest was oblivious to my sense of overwhelm. I muttered something to excuse myself and made my exit to find the nearest dark corner to fulfill my baby's needs. As I sat in a fold-out chair in the sporting goods section so Bentley could play with the soccer balls while I took care of Weston, the question kept circling through my mind:

Lady, what in the hell am I going to miss from this stage?

You see, having only one kid had been a breeze for both Mike and me. We had the perfect, textbook Gerber baby every parent wishes for. During my first maternity leave, I napped when Bentley napped, which gave me the energy to clean and cook while he played in the afternoon. Our freezer overflowed with homemade buns, cookies, and freezer meals. I returned to my pre-pregnancy weight only three months after his birth, then reduced my goal weight by another ten pounds.

Returning to my full-time corporate job after my maternity leave with Bentley felt natural, and I surpassed my expectations in both roles—boss babe and mommy extraordinaire. I was *never* late for work, and my projects were applauded for their creativity and efficient attention to detail. I was at the top of my game, hitting home runs left, right, and center.

As a family, we enjoyed evening walks to the park on a daily basis, guaranteeing time for the play and snuggles I'd missed while Bentley was in daycare. I walked the dogs twice a day—once in the morning and then again after Bentley went to bed. I had little to no mommy guilt then. Why would I? I was Mother-of-the-Year, doing and succeeding at *all* the things.

Then life exploded.

Two years after Bentley's birth, months prior to having our second son, we acquired a trucking business on top of our full-time jobs. *Boom, crackle, pop!* It was like setting fireworks off in the middle of our living room.

When Weston arrived, his needs took us by complete surprise, teaching us the true meaning of *boss baby*. His first year of life broke us in as parents—or maybe just broke us. He thrived on little sleep and refused to eat anything other than milk with a side of soother.

Mike would get up with him at night, but I was the only parent at home during the day. Out of desperation and against Mike's parenting decrees, I accommodated Weston's every demand, trying to lessen his constant bellows.

You'd like to sleep with us for the next three years? Yes, sir, please join. You'd like to drink milk all day and not consume food? Sure. You'd like to haul around your soother until you're sixteen? Absolutely.

Gone were the daily trips to the park, the Instagram-worthy snuggles, and the perfect routine. My Mother-of-the-Year trophy collected dust in a forgotten closet.

I was in survival mode. I had to remind myself daily whether it was Monday or Saturday, and I often forgot my niece's and nephew's birthdays—something previously unheard of. Dry shampoo and red-eye solution brazenly appeared on my shopping list. Washing my hair and brushing my teeth? *That* became a luxury I only indulged in if I had the time between feedings and general household duties.

Weston's arrival had been like the earthquake that starts a tsunami, and I saw only one way out of the oncoming wave of destruction.

I was going to have to settle for less than perfection for the next few years. My claim-to-fame traits—flawlessness and impeccability—would have to be abruptly replaced with flexibility, imperfection, and tardiness. *Talk about a whole new way to approach life.*

And the worst of it was I thought I was alone. Very rarely did I stumble upon an honest conversation with another mom. Unlike me, nobody seemed to want to chat about their parenting flaws, their eating disorder, multiple miscarriages, or the fact that they regularly peed their pants after childbirth over an afternoon coffee date.

I'm telling ya, not a one.[1]

What they *did* want to do was flaunt everything else that *was* working. The rivalry was real for Most Creative First Birthday Cake Smash or Most Flamboyant Girls' Night Out. *Did you make your floral arrangement by hand or order it on Etsy?*

I mindlessly surfed their Perfect Mom social media profiles during the midnight hours while eating chips in my oversized men's pyjama pants, feeling utterly, completely unworthy. I didn't have the energy to compete. I hardly had enough liveliness to walk out of the door with a bra and actual pants on.

So I continued with the exhausting expectation our millennial generation promoted. I posted fake pictures displaying only the good in our lives, pushing the mess aside and angling out any of the untidy toys in the background before capturing *the perfect shot.* The rest—my emotional wounds, insecurities, and flaws—I left for another day, sweeping them under the rug for safekeeping.

But eventually, they all came out. And when they did, it was like a cyclone had picked up my life and dumped it on a yellow brick road in a place where all the rules had changed.

Dealing with my past was not a quick or painless process. Healing never is. But while the storm of new motherhood was swirling around me, something incredible and beautiful came out of it. The early years of motherhood were the messiest part of my life—but it instigated a renovation of myself at the core level, which repaired me in the most unexpected way.

Over the next four years of my journey, I went through many stages of healing before I discovered I had been wearing enchanted heels that had the ability to take me home all along.

---

1   Insert cricket sound here.

The story you are about to read describes just how mother-hood broke me—and then how it saved me. This book shows how I found balance on the Yellow Brick Road by modifying my own circus act of motherhood to work for me, and so can *you*. My hope is by reading about my journey, you'll come to understand you're not alone over there in your pyjama pants.

So, let's go see if we can rustle up some sparkly, magic heels, shall we?

Click, click, click.

CHAPTER ONE

On The Hazards of Melting a Witch

When you're holding a cup of coffee and someone bumps into you, what would you say spills out of your cup? I guarantee you'd say coffee. If the cup held tea, you'd say tea. Whatever's in the cup will spill out when it gets jarred. Obvious, right?

The same thing applies to you and what you choose to put in your own cup of life.

When an unanticipated or staggering life event happens to you, your inner contents will come barreling out of you—passion, love, anxiety, elation, fear. In my opinion, getting hit with an unfortunate or shocking life event is the best way to measure how well you're doing on the inside.

This truth hit me hard on the morning of an unplanned province-wide power outage in the dead of winter in 2018.

For most people, a few hours without power in a Saskatchewan December isn't a major cause for alarm. More than that and you start to worry about freezing water lines and finding enough blankets, but you can manage in a sealed house for a few hours, especially in the middle of the night when the family is tucked into their beds asleep.

For me, however, at that point in my life, it was cause for a full-on anxiety attack.

With limited battery power, I couldn't mindlessly scroll social media. I couldn't cocoon in my office with the safety of Excel spreadsheets and my floor heater. I couldn't distract myself with TV, vacuuming, and laundry. I didn't even have enough natural light to read a book.

Damn the modern world.

With Mike beside me, I huddled on my bed in the cold darkness of the predawn hours and fought the panic that wanted to steal my breath, trying to keep it together for the sake of our little boys in the next room. But there was nothing to divert my attention from the muddle of my life.

My anxiety attack wasn't about the power outage, though. The contents of my cup were spilling over with mistrust, suspicion, and cynicism—feelings I'd been harbouring through years of undealt-with wounds and stress.

The ironic thing was, from the outside, it must have looked as if I was succeeding at everything I touched. I was the mom who sent fresh-baked cupcakes to school parties, I had a corporate job that funded lavish travel opportunities, and I ran a successful trucking business with my husband.

But from the inside, things were ballooning out of control, ready to burst at any moment. I had lost my voice in all aspects of my life—at work especially—and I didn't know how to dig myself out of the hole I was in. The hours I spent as a bookkeeper and accountant for our trucking business on top of my nearly full-time work-from-home corporate day job took their toll. In addition, Mike's job and long hours away from home required me to act as a single parent to our two young boys on most days. Life was bursting at the seams.

On an emotional level, bitterness from my miscarriages three years earlier still lingered above me like a dark cloud. Resentment and anger from teenage emotional wounds held me in a firm grip. At fourteen, I began turning to food to help me avoid hard emotions and would then purge the emotional calories I consumed.

Over the next fourteen years of my food addiction, I'd tried to change so many times, but my shame always won. Getting help would mean I was weak. So, despite progress I'd made in other areas over the years, the destructive cycle still continued, like a snake eating its own tail. But a snake's body is only so long, and I was running out of room to allow the cycle to continue much longer. *What if the snake ate its entire body, including its head, vanishing into thin air? What if there was nothing of me left to give?*

To make matters worse, a month before the power outage, Mike and I had received news that had the potential to impact us for years to come—our business had been embroiled in a legal matter. At the same time, the corporation I worked for was going through structural changes, which meant my future at my day job could potentially be up in the air.

We felt completely helpless. Behind the scenes, people were making decisions that could disrupt our livelihoods and there was little we could do about it. We were waiting mice in a cat's game.

Now, this cold, dark morning in December was the final straw in a heavy pile of burdens that snapped the rope I'd been using to hold my reality together. I was Dorothy trying to get myself and my little dog home, and all I could hear was the insane cackling of my past.

I had no idea what to do.

You never expect the moment that cracks you open. But when it comes, you're left staring at the pieces of yourself, wondering if all the king's horses and all the king's men can put you back together again.

I lived a fairly wholesome childhood. I'd been raised in the heart of Saskatchewan on a mixed farming operation—probably quite similar to the Kansas prairie of Dorothy's youth you might imagine. I spent my summer days bale hopping and taking long bike rides down dusty graveled roads under wide open prairie skies. Picking raspberries out of the bushes to make jam preserves for the winter months was an anticipated event every fall.

I hadn't a care or worry in the world. Why should I? My parents did my worrying for me. They guarded me from every evil they could think of, raising me in a bubble of safety. And they succeeded. I had no experience with real pain or suffering until well into adulthood.

But that naive Past Me died when I was twenty-eight years old.

Two miscarriages, occurring within months of each other between our sons, Bentley and Weston, sent me into a state of complete despair. I often refer to the time as to when

Humpty Dumpty

fell off

the wall

and cracked

open.

After my miscarriages, I was at the lowest point I had ever been emotionally. I wouldn't say I hit rock bottom, but I hardened like a boiled egg, galvanizing my emotions behind an unbreakable outer shell. Even at the time, I recognized there were so many worse things I could have gone through. However, after my losses, I haunted the self-help and healing aisles of my local Indigo bookstore.

Our first pregnancy with Bentley had been incredibly smooth, and I had anticipated our second pregnancy to be just as effortless—nothing in my past experience told me to expect otherwise. My whole life, I'd worked hard and luck had clung to my coattails in whatever I did.

When we decided to try for our second child, we became pregnant within a month. We felt so fortunate. I was never one to keep secrets well and openly shared our excitement with our families as soon as we discovered we were expecting.

Early in the pregnancy, I was at work preparing for a conference call when a stab of pain pierced my lower abdomen. I had a few minutes before my next conference call would begin, so I quickly went to the washroom to "deal with the situation." It was a moment I'd remember forever. I wasn't having stomach pains—I was in the beginning stages of a miscarriage.

I sat in the bathroom stall in disbelief, trying to comprehend that something in my life might not go right. *How could this happen to me? I'm perfectly healthy. I'm a good person. Why would God choose to impose pain on someone like me?*

Regardless, *this* situation couldn't happen right now—I had a conference call to catch. The drama would have to wait. If I ignored the symptoms, perhaps the problem would resolve itself anyway. That's what I would do. I'll get up off this toilet, go back to my desk, and—

And then it happened.

Before I could make another emotional appeal to the divine, I miscarried. Alone, in complete shock, in a crummy and unmemorable bathroom stall.

And because we do silly things when we're in shock, I did the most rational thing I could think of. I wiped my salty, heartbroken tears with no-brand toilet paper and walked back to the steadiest thing in my life—my desk—stumbling through a group of colleagues on my way into my office. I tucked the tissue and my emotions into my pocket, as per usual, and sat on a two-hour conference call. *There are more important things to worry about.*

To avoid thinking about that tissue, I asked questions throughout the entire meeting. The system we were trying to implement at work seemed extravagantly more imperative than my own health. The other participants had no idea what had happened moments ago. Goes to show that we never really know what someone's dealing with, do we?

I soon began to refer to the situation as an *incident*—merely a tiny setback in my timeline of life goals. Without hesitation, we started trying to have a baby again. I had a plan in place and that was all there was to it.

To our surprise, we became pregnant almost immediately after the miscarriage—so quickly, my doctor couldn't even place a proper due date. Again, we happily announced we were expecting to our families. I could wipe my hands clean of the last episode and pretend it didn't happen. I would sweep it under the rug, like all the other secrets in my life.

However, our strategies don't always go as planned, do they?

Seven weeks later, I miscarried again. I sat in the same public washroom, tears dripping down my cheeks, pleading to God in the lonely bathroom stall as I stared at the evidence that the worst had begun. *I'll go to church more. I'll donate to charities. I'll volunteer my time more. I'll do anything if you save my baby. You took the last one, but you can't have this one. You can't take two.*

But there was nothing I could do.

No amount of begging could stop the bleeding. I choked back my tears so the women outside the stall couldn't hear my whimpers. It didn't matter that I was falling apart—I refused to show my emotions beyond the one-inch-thick door two feet in front of me. I had to walk a straight line somewhere, and that somewhere was most definitely the office. Not knowing what else to do, I did what I knew best—I went back to work.

You don't get to fall apart now. Not here. After all, I still had to pick up Bentley. I had to encounter numerous people to get from my desk to the daycare and through our front door. That's where I could finally break down. That's when I could feel the reality of the situation—when no one was looking—and not a minute before.

So I endured another afternoon of meetings, trying to ignore my cramping abdomen. Then I mindlessly collected Bentley and buckled him in, thankful his car seat was directly behind mine so he wouldn't see the tears falling from my chin.

I gripped the steering wheel to steady myself. *It will be better soon.* I'd called Mike to leave work early and meet me at home. I would soon be able to collapse in his embrace. And even though I knew the inevitable outcome, I kept making deals with God. *Maybe it was just bleeding. Maybe the baby would be spared.*

My prayers went unanswered.

I stood in our bathroom, staring at the teary-eyed reflection in the mirror. Mike was just outside the door, and I knew he'd feel disappointment, too. But for the most part, I would be alone in the emotional journey ahead.

I was no longer in my safe prairie state of Kansas. I was displaced, confused, and homesick for the life I once knew. *What was I supposed to do now?* I had to be brave and happy for our one baby that was alive, my Bentley. He needed someone to hold him, to love him, and to pretend like nothing out of the ordinary had changed his mother forever.

I dried my tears, exited the bathroom and told Mike what had happened, then went to the kitchen and began pulling out mixing bowls and ingredients.

"What are you doing?" he asked.

"I'm making cake."

He watched me for a moment, then let me be.

The week prior, I had promised my niece I would make her a birthday cake for her party that weekend. Numbly, I realized I could wallow or make cake—so cake it was. I spent the evening whipping the batter with my grief. Tears and anger rolled themselves into the kneaded princess pink fondant. I topped the cake with sprinkles and purple buttercream frosting before calling it a day.

A deep seed of sadness formed within me that night. My broken heart drew a debilitating dark cloud around me. It was the first time I was not completely sheltered from the hardness of life.

Since everyone had known we were expecting again, I would eventually have to tell them the updated news. After they found out, I would burst into tears anytime someone brought up condolences. No one knew what to say, not even Mike. No one knew what would set me off.

I blamed myself for both miscarriages. Trying to make sense of it all, I grasped at possible causes with a long list of *what ifs.*

Because if I knew what had caused them, I could prevent it from happening again, right?

What if it's all of the travel I've been doing over the last few months, or that martini in Manhattan before I knew I was pregnant? What if it's the workouts I was doing or because I fell while walking the dogs? What if it's the protein shakes I've been drinking? Could there be something dangerous in the ingredient list?

I had spent my entire life trying to lose weight. What if it was *me*? What if trying to stay fit and healthy during the pregnancy had actually caused my loss?

Every time I heard about another woman who conceived easily or, worse yet, had an unplanned pregnancy, I was overcome with bitterness. *Why does she get a baby if she doesn't even want one?*

I was irate with God, having more fear of his plan than faith in his supposed goodness. *Why on earth would someone ever cause this to happen to us intentionally?* I yelled into the void. *What was the purpose in this?*

When I couldn't find the right words or answers, I turned to quotes. One night, huddled under my bed covers routinely surfing social media feeds, I found a quote meme by an unknown author that would change my perspective forever. It suggested that when things in your life seem to be falling apart, they might actually be falling into place. It was the first thing that made me feel better, and I clung to it, holding it to my heart in the middle of the night. It became my beacon of hope and gave me direction when I had no place to turn, leading me out of a dark place of anger and making me look at my situation through a new lens. *The universe might be working behind the scenes to create an even better plan than before.*

Shortly after the second miscarriage, I spoke to my older sister, Jennifer, on the phone.

"How can I ever try to get pregnant?" I wailed into the receiver. "Why would I intentionally put myself through that much pain again?"

"But at least you can try," she said in response. "Some of us don't even have that chance."

I stopped short. At a young age, Jennifer had learned she could not carry her own children. She was being a supportive big sister when she probably wanted to slap me silly.

Her response changed my entire outlook on my state of affairs.

I wiped my tears and gathered my composure. *It's time to wake up, girly girl.*

At least we can try became my mantra. I repeated it to myself when the pregnancy test came back negative the next month. And then, to my surprise, positive the month after. I repeated it to myself as the weeks rolled by and we passed first seven, then nine, then the dreaded twelve-week mark on the calendar and I started to breathe a little easier. *Maybe this baby will live. Maybe the risk was worth it.*

The mantra resulted in the birth of our second son, Weston. I don't know if I would have chanced another heartache without that encouraging phone call. (Weston, if you are reading this, you can thank your Aunty JJ for your existence.)

The experience of cracking open left me floundering, searching for the reasons behind why we as humans suffer at all. I questioned God: *Is our suffering a part of a higher evolution process? Is our healing to be used as an empathic aid towards the next human travelling with grief?* Ultimately, I found more questions to ask the Big Guy when I get back up there than I ever found answers to.

My anger with the Father, the Son, and the Holy Spirit caused a spiritual rift in my heart, so I did not invite God to join me on my initial healing journey. I was raised to believe in him, but I felt

God had failed me in my time of need. I had to find something else to hold on to, so I looked for hope beyond my Christian faith.

Because some questions cannot be answered by Google, I explored *anything* that made me feel better, including forms of holistic energy healing practices. Feathers, crystals, and smudge herbs occupied my living space, while new forms of spirituality filled my heart space—daily meditations and yoga became spiritual pillars during this time. Expanding my definition and belief system around God expedited my exit from the dark tunnel of grief I was in.

By the time Bentley was five and Weston was two, it was how I found myself sitting in a weekend healing course with a medicine woman several years after the miscarriages and only seven months before that fateful power outage. It was at that session when I finally started addressing some of the limiting beliefs that had been holding me back—my anger issues, resentment towards others, and the grief I'd been pushing away for years. For the first time, I could see the possibility of forgiveness, and I took my first hopeful, wobbly steps towards it.

My miscarriages broke me, but instead of allowing myself to heal, I had become hard, ignoring the pain it caused. By the time I attended that weekend healing session, I was tired of being a rigid, broken vessel. I was ready to move on.

During the course, she'd seen a vision of me writing, which I dismissed at the time. But as the doors of my heart opened, it seemed I was learning new and profound lessons on a daily basis. Four months later, I started my blog and began what I now call my Year of Writing and Rebranding. I started openly talking about my miscarriages, and I found I was not alone. In fact, I was startled to find out how high the miscarriage rate is. So many women who responded to my story had gone through similar experiences.

I was comforted to know so many others were dealing, or had dealt, with the same emotional issues. When I learned I wasn't singled out, I placed less blame on myself for being the cause of my losses. *Perhaps it wasn't me at all?*

When it happened to me, I had no one to relate to. I had to force open the doors for others to join in the conversation. I was a new mom, and those were topics we didn't touch on during mundane coffee dates. I didn't have a regular therapist to talk to. Rather foolishly, I sat with those emotions for years before I actually dealt with them.

Hearing so many stories like mine made me wonder why miscarriages are such a taboo subject in the first place. As I had begun the healing process, my heart had not only softened, but developed more room in it. As time allowed me to absorb my own pain, I also gained empathy for the women who followed a similar storyline to me.

Now, I share this story with you for a few reasons. I want to open the door for you to process your own losses or provide a resource if you ever need to walk through a similar healing process. I want to dedicate this story to all of the mothers who have walked a similar fate and to all who have survived the journey. I want to acknowledge the women who have endured loss, who have carried loss, or have given birth to loss. To the mothers who have had children, who have raised them, and who have lost them. Losing a child is a difficult process and I want to acknowledge you here.

Most importantly, this is a love letter to the babies I'll never know, but who I'll always remember. Your tiny but profound imprints allowed me to grow into something much bigger and better than ever before.

Most of us wait for a crisis before we change—at least I did.

Real awakening wasn't an elegant process—it was actually the furthest thing from it. It was messy, ugly, raw, and shattering. My stable environment had shifted, cracking my eggshell wide open. The shards lay in pieces on the pavement, leaving me completely exposed and falling apart.

Cracking open made me see how lost I had become over the past ten years. I had played by the rules, becoming extremely disciplined and serious as a young adult. I had taken the exact roads suggested in my imaginary book of *How to be Successful in Life*.

By the time I was twenty-five years old, I'd acquired a university degree, a budding career, a mortgage, and a marriage. By the time I was twenty-eight, my husband and I had added our trucking business and two babies to the mix. We had a retirement savings plan that guaranteed if we made it to the age of sixty, we'd never have to worry about money, and neither would our children. We were confident in the choices we made in our twenties . . . or so we thought.

Up to that point, the part of my life I had been most proud of was my corporate job in the city supporting a sales staff across western Canada for an agriculture company. I was a somebody inside those office walls, which I decorated with high achievement awards and professional designation certificates. I sat in boardrooms with intelligent people, assisting them on projects that had the potential to shape the face of agriculture. I felt purpose in my job, as if I were contributing to something greater than just myself.

While I focused on creating a successful career, I set aside *everything* else. After convocation from university, I thought that carrying a black briefcase and being very serious about life were my keys to victory. So I wore the business-approved black heels. I carried the perfect, black briefcase. I thought I had made it.

But something was wrong. Something felt off. In my quest to have a career, status, and money, I had stopped playing music. *Who has time for music? I have a career to build!*

This new version of myself was so far away from who I used to be that I almost didn't recognize myself. Music had once been like medicine to me. In my younger years—before I found that blasted imaginary book—I used to dance half-naked to salsa music in the morning, just because it felt good. But as I started following my new formula for success, small pleasures like dancing got pushed aside. I didn't even listen to the salsa music anymore. I kept telling myself I'd create a new music playlist as soon as I had everything in order. But the years kept passing and I kept procrastinating—life wasn't *perfect* yet.

I had traded many hours of happiness for a job that now overtook my family life. I was no longer enjoying the pursuit of success as I had once imagined it. I had majored in economics in university, and, in my current position, the classic cost-benefit analysis rang true—the benefits provided by my job were no longer outweighing the costs.

Clearly, I was lost.

Yes, I had investments and extravagant travel experiences notched in my belt, but I was desperately lonely. I had no close friendships. Looking back at my twenties, I could see how isolated and monotonous they had actually been. And now, I was tired of the hustle and bustle *all of the time*. Mike and I fantasized about leaving the country just to get a break from our commitments for one week.

Once I returned to work after my maternity leave with Weston, I began to question the paradigm I had created. In my corporate climb to career success, I had failed to see how ill-tempered and unhappy I had become. Beyond work, I had nothing meaningful to show for myself. After experiencing loss with the miscarriages, I saw how limited time could be. I couldn't wait for the *right* moment any longer. What if perfection never came?

I packed up all of the trophies and certificates that bordered my desk and barricaded those accomplishments in my desk drawer. I still had my job, but now my desk—and my life—were open to new opportunities, ones I would find more meaningful. It was if I had a blank canvas to begin with.

When Mike signed up for a music service subscription not long after my cleaning session, I nearly toppled him over while grabbing my phone to try it out. Mike was confused over the intensity of my excitement, and I don't blame him. He had no idea the significance behind what I was doing. After so many years of neglecting my own joy, the music playlist was my first embarkation on my journey of change and restoration. It felt like I was in the beginning stages of creating a new life, not just a playlist. I planned to start building the best version of myself immediately, one song at a time.

I signed into his online music account, ready to begin adding songs to my new Happy List. I paused, thinking back to the last time I actually *felt* happy with music playing in the background, and the verses of "Tiny Dancer" by Elton John started playing in my head. *That's it, I've got the first one!* After downloading my first song, I branched out, actively seeking out new songs that were current on the radio.

Music brought magic back into our home, and dance parties became regular occurrences. Weston had so much fun with them, he'd even go one step further with *naked* dance parties, including a few twerk movements.[2] I felt happier, the kids felt happier, we *all* felt happier—and that little taste of happiness made me want more.

Not wanting to waste any more time stuck in misery, I wrote out a list of items I wanted to fix in my life—or someone's life, anyway. I bow my head in embarrassment over the ignorance that inspired my initial Fix-It List. It appeared in order to find the solution to my problem, I would need to change everyone around me.

I can now see that my need to rescue, fix, and change others was a huge indicator of how much I needed my own self-restoration project. My judgements and criticisms were merely diversions from my own inner work, and the only one who needed to change was *me*. I needed to melt an inner witch, not repair the internal workings of other villains around me.

The problem was, I was delving into unknown territory with my deep excavation project, bringing to the surface feelings I didn't know how to properly sift through. I didn't know how to feel raw emotions because I had trained myself to eat them away. Food was a beautiful crutch. To fully heal, I'd have to tackle the most wicked part of me, my eating disorder. I'd have to address the reasons behind why it started, and *those* were feelings I'd rather leave tucked away. It seemed easier that way, especially now that I saw how difficult emotions could be to manage.

Kintsugi is the Japanese art of repairing a broken piece of pottery with golden metal, leaving visible veins of gold behind. The philosophy is that the piece is more beautiful for having been broken—the true essence of the bowl begins the moment it is dropped and cracked.†

---

2   Although sometimes tempting, Mike, Bentley, and I did not join in on Weston's lack of clothing preference.

I was the Humpty Dumpty of broken pottery, an egg laying on the ground in pieces, and I knew it.

But I *wanted* to be a woman repaired with gold, vividly shining for the world to see. Little did I know, I *had* to crack open to clearly see all of my flaws. And the precious metal required to mend me would come from lessons inspired by the most unexpected of sources—my children.

CHAPTER TWO

"Did I Just Get Hit by a Flying House?"

Becoming a mother wasn't a natural process for me. You would have never caught me playing with baby dolls and fantasizing about singing a lullaby to an actual baby. A farm cat dressed in play clothes, maybe, but *never* a baby.

No, I had a Barbie doll who would shop for pink high heels for her next social event or drive to the pool party next door in her convertible. *My* Barbie was making out with Ken on the couch in the basement room of the doll house where her mom wouldn't catch her. Sometimes, she'd leave the house to go to work across town (which meant driving to the other Barbie house across our playroom). I always stopped short of Barbie and Ken having a baby and starting a family. All I really wanted was the glitz and glamour, and none of the domestic bliss.

I weaseled out of any babysitting job my mother tried to sign me up for in my teenage years by pretending I was sick. The idea of playing hide-and-seek paralyzed me with boredom. Interacting with children didn't feel like my calling. Organizing volunteers for school events or prioritizing projects on the school social committee—*those* were my calling.

My maturity level at the age of twenty when I fell in love with Mike, who was twenty-two, wasn't too far advanced from when I left high school. We were married at the ripe old ages of twenty-four and twenty-six, and neither of us had any idea of what we were getting into.

When we said our *I dos*, we were more concerned about what kind of champagne and strawberries we would have prepared at our honeymoon suite in Maui than about our married life that would soon follow. *Will the strawberries be dipped in white or dark chocolate? And do they really greet you with leis once the plane lands?*

Before long, Mike and I jumped blindly into starting a family. After marriage, getting pregnant sounded like the perfect next step. The whole thing sounded so romantic: you, me, and baby makes three. Why wouldn't I want in on that?

And of course I'd be the perfect mother and my children would be looked upon by other mothers with envy. *If only my Charlotte were as well-behaved and talented as your little Averie*, they'd say, and I'd modestly demur with, *I'd be happy to give you pointers.* (Because, you see, I planned only to have girls. Boys were out of the question.)

Please feel free to snort coffee out of your nose.

Before I became a mother, I was an expert at rearing children. I mentally shamed the parents who frantically ran into the office an hour late, disordered and ruffled. I didn't understand why they looked so tired or why there was no bounce in their step. *Come on, people, we have projects to produce, hop to it! Coffee machine is on your left . . .*

One day, my colleagues and I were having a regular lunch meeting outside of the office walls and decided to carpool. In order to fit everyone into my colleague's four-door vehicle, she had to move her car seats into the trunk. As she lugged the contraptions to the back, crumbs and McDonald's wrappers scattered across the parking lot.

I discreetly peeked into the back of the car and noticed morsels of leftovers in every crevice. The mounds of old fries and toys would have made interesting material for an archeological dig. I gingerly cleared off the seat before sitting down and buckling up. My colleague, noticing nothing out of ordinary, hopped in the driver's seat and off we went.

Upon arriving at the restaurant, I hopped out of the backseat to find a remnant of the car ride stuck to my bum—a whole Cheerio. I carefully picked if off without the group noticing, yet walked away judging the mess in the car and the mom driving it. *When I become a mother, I'll never let my kids eat in the car.*

It was only the latest of many "when I become a mother" pronouncements I had made to myself over the years as I self-righteously sniffed at other parents. Boy, did I have a lot to learn. (Trust me, I'm rolling my eyes as I write this admission, too.)

From that day on, I privately referred to this woman as the Cheerio Lady. I am now appalled that I judged her about her messy car. Now that I sign school permission slips with the nearest Crayola crayon or smelly marker—and my own car looks like a survivor of the *Clone Wars*—I can fully empathize with her.

But when Mike and I first said the words *let's have a baby*, I didn't know any of that. No one could have prepared me for the job I was signing up for—mostly because I wouldn't have listened. Honestly, I probably wouldn't have even asked the question. As per usual, I got an idea in my head and went full steam ahead toward it. Just over a year after we tied the knot, we were trying to get pregnant.

You know when you buy a new car and suddenly it seems you're seeing that make and model everywhere you go? Trying to become pregnant is a bit like that.

Or maybe it's more like being infatuated. You know what you want, but you have no idea that the real fun is in dreaming about it. Once you have it, it becomes *work*.

I saw pregnant women wherever I went. My day was filled with romanticized ideas of how wonderful motherhood would be. I designed the perfect plan—the baby would be born in summer and we could go for daily walks with the stroller to melt away my maternity weight.

And, of course, that's how it went. Like most things in my life to that point, my pregnancy with Bentley was precisely executed, and he arrived in July.

Despite the way everything kept falling into place, when we conceived so quickly, my mind started to race with all of the unknowns. I mean, I had never changed a diaper before. The closest I had come to caring for a baby prior to having my own was when my sister-in-law set my niece on me five years earlier, expecting me to feed her. I had no choice *but* to hold her—it was me or the floor.

I stared at the mushed food in front of me, and started sweating profusely at the idea of being responsible for feeding a tiny human being. *Was I seriously prepared to care for my own baby? Isn't there some sort of interview process I should have to go through prior to becoming a parent?*

My mother, bless her, looked terrified when I told her we were expecting. She knew what I was like—selfish, inexperienced, and young. To her credit, when I would spout off with some novice comment about what my idealized version of motherhood would be like, she would bite her lip and speak only with caution, or not at all. Looking back, I can only imagine how much self-discipline this took.

As her third child, I'd had it made in the shade. My oldest sister, Pamela, had held the majority of responsibilities around the house, helping to take care of us and creating the cleaning list each Saturday morning. I swear my current habit of creating to-do lists originated from watching her do this.

Next in line was Jennifer, my second sister, who served time for us all. She was grounded most of the time, and I think she wore out my parents. By the time they got to me and my little brother, they were tired. *Stop asking questions and just go watch cartoons…*

Whether I'd learned from Jennifer's example or was just more compliant, I don't know, but I was the type of kid you never had to enforce rules for. I obeyed them religiously without being asked. However, I also didn't take any responsibility for my younger brother, Mike. (Yes, another Mike. I'm surrounded.) For the most part, thanks to my good-girl persona, I was free to pursue my own interests, which left me remarkably self-centered as I stepped into adulthood.

The habit of caring only about myself didn't magically disappear when I moved out of my parents' house at eighteen. On one of my classic to-do lists from my early twenties, it was standard to see items like *nap, read, walk, nails,* and *wax* listed for an average Saturday afternoon.

Little did that naive, inexperienced Past Me know that those would soon become luxuries reserved for those who didn't spend the majority of their day cleaning up the various and voluminous (seriously, how do babies produce so much?) forms of liquids created by a miniature human body.

When I was about to return to work after my maternity leave with Bentley, I asked my friend, a veteran working mom, how she fit laundry into her schedule. *She must have a designated laundry day, like each Tuesday, to do it all at one time.* Smiling, she meekly replied she did it whenever it needed to be done—like it was something that was sometimes finished and she could start again when necessary, but the requirement to do so was surely a rare event. What she didn't say was that it would need to be done every day without fail and that trying to fit it all into a single day per week would have not been possible.

I wish she would have been honest. I went away from that conversation with rose-tinted glasses on. *I've got this—being a working mom will be as easy as one, two, three. I can still do* all *the things.* Honestly, I had no idea what I was getting into. No one told me parenting while working could sometimes feel like you were about to be blindsided by a flying house.

Now, if a newbie ever asks me what it's like to be a working mom, I'm upfront about it. It isn't all roses, period. My usual warning goes somewhat like this: "You know how the house looks when the family has been sick for a week—dirty laundry everywhere, an untidy and disorganized mess? Being a working mom is sort of like that, but the messiness *never ends.* Oh, and you never feel well-rested at work, you are constantly guilt-ridden from daycare drop-offs, and you eat on the go a *lot.* That should give you a good start on envisioning it."[3]

---

3   This is, of course, my opinion only. But guess what? I'm usually given accolades from new working moms when we look back to our original conversation. They thank me for my honesty around the realities of entering the workforce with babies.

And because I work, laundry can take up to five business days to complete. I've gotten a lot less particular about how it gets done since having kids, too. Everything gets thrown in together—cottons, towels, underwear, darks, and whites (or, um, *pinks*)—there is no sorting over here.

Once the rinse cycle ends, the load might sit in the washer overnight or until I remember it's there. The same happens after the dryer cycle. An evening or two later, it gets thrown into a full laundry basket of clean clothes. Folding laundry? Who has time for that? (Except my Lululemon gear—*those* items always take precedence.)[4]

As you can imagine, our clean clothes basket tends to accumulate in strength over time. When our drawers are empty and my boys are wearing socks with holes in them (you know, the reserve ones in the back of the drawer), I know I *must* fold and put away the laundry so I can stop directing my kids to the clean hamper to grab their clothes for the day. (Don't tell my mother-in-law.)

My chaotic laundry process is an exact correlation to what it sometimes feels like to be a mother—everlasting and exhausting. Although the clothes are clean, they are in a disorganized heap and there is always a basket waiting to be folded and put away.

As I was folding clothes one day when Weston was about two, and before I'd discovered that a music playlist makes the job go faster (my playlist still had only a few songs on it), I found a wrinkled red shirt at the bottom of the heap. The colour was faded, the material worn out, and the collar ruffled and stretched. As I tried

---

4   I don't always have time to fold and put away the laundry, but even when I do, I don't. I despise it, and so does Mike. Whenever I throw around the idea of having a third child, Mike's immediate argument is the fact that we'll have more laundry to do. And that does it—he wins "the discussion" every time. Two it is!

to coax that unfortunate garment into a semblance of neatness, I realized that *I* was the red shirt, wrinkled and worn out, but trying to stay in one piece, fulfilling my intended purpose.

Then I made another startling observation about my laundry-folding process.

As I worked, I put away my oldest son's pyjamas, my other son's shirts, my husband's underwear, and even the dish towels before I ever touched any of my own laundry. I had unintentionally put everyone else's clothes away before mine. And that's how I did it *every time*.

As a new mom, I was stuck under a heap of responsibilities I was pretending weren't suffocating me. And the laundry lineup—from most important to least important—was a microcosm of how I was treating myself as a young mom. I put myself last in every aspect of my life. I had recognized I was doing it to some extent, but until that moment I hadn't realized it was tumbling right down to my underwear and socks.

Terrified of becoming the inferior mother I assumed my mother had anticipated I would become, I had done everything in my power to prove otherwise. I trained myself to let go of my own bare necessities in order to claim the title of Mommy Extraordinaire. While following my idea of what it meant to raise children adequately, I had lost myself completely.

The next week as I was doing laundry, I took baby steps to change the way I prioritized myself. After folding and sorting, I put away my items first.

It was *extremely* difficult. Putting myself first was a preposterous idea. *How dare I?*

To this day, I still have the urge to put everyone else's items away before my own. I have to mentally prepare myself before I sort laundry. *It's just laundry, and I'm worthy, too. My underwear is just as important as Bentley's. Why is this even an argument in my head right now?* To this day and as a mother, the struggle to put myself first is real.

Shortly after that laundry episode, I began to think deeply about what I wanted out of life. I had built a playlist of music to make me happy, but I still felt anything but happy in so many areas of my life—especially in my career. *Am I happy with what I've chosen to do with my time here on Earth? Do I actually like what I do for a living, or is it simply a paycheque? Where would I like to be in five years mentally, physically, and socially?* I asked myself those questions every day, searching my heart for the truth.

In blogger and motivational speaker Rachel Hollis's book *Girl, Wash Your Face*, she addresses the priorities of women like me. When she asked women to name the things on their priority list, they seemed to be able to write down their items with complete ease—kids, partner, work, faith, etc. The order of the listed items sometimes changed, but the bullet points rarely did. More often than not, the lists did not contain a bullet point for themselves. Women prioritized caring for everyone else, but they were so low on their own lists that they didn't even get mentioned.‡

I'll let you breathe that in.

Reading that passage left me speechless, staring at the page in her book for a long while. I, too, was nowhere near a bullet point on my own list. I was a faded, tired, and worn-out version of my old self. Gone were the days when I'd list to-dos like *hair, wax, pilates,* or *nails.* My lists now regularly featured *laundry, make supper, walk dogs, purchase birthday gift,* and *pay bills.*

Oh, how my life had changed—and my lists knew it before I did.

My grocery lists adapted to my new life without even asking. Wine and ricotta cheese had stepped aside for baby formula, diapers, and apple sauce. There was nothing on the list for me—unless you count hemorrhoid cream and Depends pads. (And I'd rather not dwell on the reasons those were on there in the first place.)

Placing self-care items on my list became my first attempt at prioritizing myself again. I added *lift weights*, *read book*, *jog*, and *paint nails* back onto my checklist and stared at it, guilt tugging at me. But I left them there, and often checked some of those items off.

Any time remorse began to bubble to the surface, I reminded myself of the airplane safety introduction I had so frequently endured during my business trips just a few short years before.

In order to lift off and pull away from Earth's gravitational force, you must listen to a short set of safety demonstrations by airline attendants who kindly remind you that if an issue arises—you know, like debris striking a jet engine or an internal system component failure—the oxygen masks will immediately release from the ceiling cabinet for your safety. The flight attendant demonstrates the correct way to tighten the air mask straps across your face and insists that you must put on your own breathing mask first—even before assisting small children. That selfish act of helping yourself first is actually how you have the ability to help others next. You're not much help unconscious on the floor, now are you?

Let me tell it to you straight, momma bear—if you're not breathing, neither are your babies. And in order to survive motherhood, you need to know where your oxygen mask is stored at all times. You need to know the various forms your mask comes in—jogging, knitting, reading, cooking, taking a weekend away, whatever nurtures your mental health.

And another thing—nobody is going to know you need saving unless you ask. It's up to you to save yourself. We're all struggling to keep up with the busyness of life. Very rarely will someone reach out and see if you're needing help or add you to their already daunting to-do list unless you say something.

Here's a great example for you: My first planned revision schedule for this book fell in the month of December. As the date my editor would return my unfinished manuscript to me approached, I was in the midst of holiday socials galore. Invites inundated my inbox—Christmas concerts and parties, birthday gatherings, girls' nights out. My calendar looked like it had caught the chicken pox. I was exhausted just looking at the month ahead. *Heaven forbid one of kids ends up getting sick. There's no time.* (By the way, my entire family went down with the flu the last week of December. Never test the fates . . .)

On top of the looming event schedule, I still had my day job to be accountable for, as well as the bookkeeping and invoicing for our trucking business. Pretending I had time to fit in hockey practice, homework, and sugar cookies left me feeling exhausted. And, guess what? No helpful little elves came knocking at my door to assist in the chaos. If I was going to get through the month and not miss any of our commitments, I needed a plan. So here's what I did:

I asked for help.

I outsourced my cleaning for the month of December. I prioritized and declined a few invites. I took every ounce of responsibility off of my plate to ensure I'd have time for my manuscript when it arrived from my editor. I bought and wrapped all of my Christmas gifts before the month even began. Once I got the manuscript back, I used the last of my annual vacation days to give me time away from my day job. Weston attended daycare for a couple additional days to give me time to focus on writing without his constant questions and interruptions. I asked my husband to take time off work to assist with daycare pickup and birthday party drop-offs. I asked my mother-in-law to take the boys for a sleepover.

Self-care came in the form of writing this book and nothing was stopping me from finishing it. In order to fulfill my dream, I called in the village to assist.

Again, let me tell it to you straight—you can make excuses, or you can make priorities. And if you're serious about getting something done, or creating a better life for that matter, you'll find a way. It's just the way passion works. You don't have to tell me what a daunting task it is to try to add another thing (i.e. yourself) into your already busting-at-the-seams schedule. I'll be honest with you—even now, I'm usually the one who falls off my to-do list at the end of the day. With that being said, I know how important it is for us mommas to continue the daily task of keeping ourselves happy.

Self-care is not a luxury—it's a necessity. And I don't care if you are young, middle-aged, or even a grand-momma bear. No matter your age, it's absolutely essential for you to be able to continue to show up in all areas of your life. You have to learn how to actively dodge the flying houses that spiral around you because when you're happy, everyone else around you will notice—family, friends, fur babies, and colleagues alike.

In my experience, if you're not diligent, self-care will be the first thing to slide off the roster in those early baby years. Similar to my experience, you might look at yourself in the mirror to see a hairy woolly mammoth looking back at you. The lack of sleep might even leave you feeling like you are siblings with the Grinch.

On the plus side, taking a bath, curling your hair, or brushing your teeth (or better yet, all three luxury items knocked off in one single morning) will leave you feeling like you've just dropped five hundred-dollar bills at the spa, amiright? And when you get to drink your coffee *hot* (or at least at a realistic lukewarm temperature) or sleep for six straight hours, aren't you in the most incredible mood for the rest of the day?

But self-care shouldn't only be about washing your hair or ensuring your nails are done. It should encompass things that let you grow emotionally, intellectually, physically, and spiritually, too.

I know what you're thinking—*I'm already run ragged by the end of the day. I'm lucky if I get myself fed and in a relatively clean shirt, let alone nurture my intellect. Who has time to grow, or read a book, for that matter? I barely have time to stream the latest episode of* Workin' Moms *on Netflix.*

I've been there, sista. After having my babies, I wanted so badly to get back into shape and feel strong again, but there were some days in the early stages of motherhood when I could barely pick myself off the floor. I had little energy or ambition for burpees and lunges after a night in the rocking chair with my teary-eyed, ravenous baby.

Know it's okay to be in the Grace Stage. If you're so sleep-deprived you start walking around looking for your coffee with your coffee in your hand, like I once did, it's time to use your extra minutes for naps, not workouts. That's self-care, too. Self-care looks different at different stages of the motherhood journey.

As a new mom, I was self-conscious and uncomfortable with my new body. I no longer had that cute baby bump tightening my belly. I wasn't able to fit into my old clothes yet and was forced to wear the stretchy yoga pants I'd worn at seven months pregnant. I would look in the mirror and feel just awful about myself.

Those were the moments I stepped back to remind myself that I was a gosh-darn superhero—I had just grown and delivered a tiny human, for goodness' sake. Those were the moments I knew to thank my body instead of forcing myself back into media's idea of health and beauty. I honoured it with the things it needed to heal—sleep and time. *Take that, society.*

It wasn't until after both of my kids started sleeping full nights that I was able to incorporate an enjoyable physical routine into my day—and it was hard to fit in even then. My daily responsibilities took precedence over my own needs on a regular basis. By the time I was through with those, I was usually dead tired—I just wanted to go to bed.

But eventually, I knew it was time to get back to my workout routine, and the only thing preventing me was making it a priority. To ensure I made it onto the to-do list, I scheduled myself into my calendar. My workout appointment became no different than any other office meeting, school event, or doctor appointment. I became fully accountable for my own health.

The concept of being healthy and preventative in my youth excites me. If I live proactively today, I won't have to be in reactive mode in the future. I envision living a long life with no medication to aid me. I see Future Me as a strong and fit eighty-year-old hiking the Grand Canyon on a moonlit tour and lifting weights in my spare time.

But I've tried to make time for myself, I hear you saying, *and there just aren't enough hours in the day.*

Let me tell you one more story that might help you. It's a story of how I made the impossible, well, possible.

When I gave birth to Bentley, my bladder lost nearly all working capacity. After Bentley spent a few days in the neonatal intensive care unit (NICU), Mike and I were ready to head home with our new family. I was standing at the foot of my hospital bed when I suddenly started to pee my pants in front of my husband. I'm not talking a little dribble when you sneeze or laugh, I mean the whole nine yards. It was the first time I had experienced anything like it.

Let me tell ya, it wasn't the fairy-tale ending I thought I'd be leaving the hospital with. I stood there in a puddle of pee, absolutely mortified.

Bentley had arrived early—our first example of how a baby shows you who the real boss is—and I still hadn't packed the hospital diaper bag because I thought I still had three weeks left to do it. (Hello, Naive Self . . .) In the excitement, poor Mikey had been left to go back home to pack items to bring to the hospital when he met me there after I went into labour, including a change of clothes for me. Unfortunately, when my bladder let go, we discovered the spare pants he'd packed for me were too small. Without a single word, Mike took off his sweat pants and kindly passed them over. (Luckily, he had also packed an extra pair for himself.)

As if giving birth weren't invasive enough, following Bentley's arrival, I continued to endure months (and *months*) of pelvic floor physiotherapy appointments. (Yup, that's right hun, lots of different hands all up in my business.) My appointment with our provincial bladder specialist to see why my case was so extreme was the pinnacle of the entire process. *Super* fun experience. (Insert sarcasm here.)

No one could really explain my case, but to put a label on the situation, the doctor determined I had an overactive bladder. I was given a prescription to try to tame it—which I later found out was the same medication my grandmother was taking. *Fantastic.*

The medication helped, but not always. And the main side effect of taking it was dry mouth. *Alrighty, if I take the pill, I stop peeing my pants, but then I'm thirsty.* Welcome to my conundrum.

Shopping at Costco became equivalent to walking the Hall of Shame for Incontinents—and even there, the carts weren't big enough for our needs. By the time I put Bentley's infant carrier (baby included), a diaper box for him, and a Depends box for me in the cart, there was no room left for groceries. *Sorry, guys, no food this week.*

To feel less ashamed of my condition, I'd tell the cashier what a wonderful granddaughter I was for picking up a large box of Depends for my grandmother. In retrospect, she probably wondered why it was so important she know that.

At one of my follow-up appointments, my specialist suggested an additional solution—no caffeine. *What kind of fresh hell have I landed in? Don't drink coffee and you'll pee yourself a little less? Are you kidding me? Does she know what it's like living with a newborn?*

I stared at the specialist with tears streaming down my face, absorbing what this could mean. The questions came flooding out: How was I ever going to sit in another boardroom surrounded by colleagues? Would I ever be able to go on another run in public? Would I have to be on this medication for the rest of my life? Would this *situation* ever resolve?

And was coffee—*my everything*—really being taken away from me?

My specialist locked her gaze with mine and took my hand. In a stern voice, she said something that I will never forget:

"Keep running. Don't let this stop you. Slap on a Depends pad and *keep running.*"

I looked at her, wiped my eyes, and nodded my head in reluctant acceptance. But as I left her office, I realized she was right. By the time I got Bentley back in the house, I had made some promises to myself.

I wouldn't let my condition barricade me away from the normal life I'd had before. I would run again one day. I would sit in a boardroom of colleagues without having to excuse myself multiple times. In time, I would figure out a way to be off the prescribed medication. (And I'd find a way to squeeze in a bit of my caffeinated drug while doing it.)

So, I continued physiotherapy appointments and started doing the recommended pelvic floor exercises with religious fervour. I took the medication, and, begrudgingly, I went off coffee temporarily.

Even though I followed all of the recommendations, I continued to pee my pants. Life went on as usual . . . except when I had to stop taking the medication when we started trying for our second child, which resulted in *more* peeing of the pants.

To avoid the public eye, I changed my jogging route to the outside of town to ensure no one I knew could see my soaked pants. I ran home in wet pants more times than I'd like to count. (I still do.) But Mike never made me feel embarrassed during those Walks of Shame to the laundry machine. The support he gave me allowed me to continue. And regardless of how much shame I felt, I held my head high and continued to put on new pants. I kept running, exactly as the doctored ordered.

A miracle happened after I gave birth to Weston. Within months, my bladder started to slowly and magically fix itself. It was as if nothing had ever happened. Well, sort of. It's not perfect, by any means, but I'd say I'm at a seventy-two percent chance of not peeing my pants every day, compared to a measly five percent when the issue first arose.

Once I figured out to cross my legs before sneezing and learned how to tighten my pelvic floor before making a big jump on a trampoline (a few tricks of the trade—you're welcome), I happily packaged up all of my Depends pads and gave them to my grandma.

At present day, there are two very bad things that can go wrong when I start a run.[5] One, my knee could pop out due to a past injury. Or two, I could potentially pee myself.

Before heading out on the trail I cross my fingers that the result will be neither, and I go for the run.

Sometimes, my knee pops out and I have to go through the process of putting it back in place by myself. (Which is as horrible and painful as it sounds.) On occasion, I can't get my knee back in place, and I've had to call Mike to pick me up while I lay waiting on the ground. And sometimes, I come home with wet pants. *Whoops. Oh, well!*

But I'd rather risk those outcomes than not be active at all. There are plenty of times I run the whole way with no problems and come home feeling as if I've won a marathon.

Those are the ones I run for.

Take it from me—a survivor—your mind is capable of more than you think.

I could have given up hope that my condition was curable. But I challenged the initial diagnosis and changed the outcome. Instead of taking medication for life, I chose to work on pelvic floor exercises. I didn't let circumstances limit my beliefs about what was possible or hinder my enjoyment of life. If I would have been deterred from going running by the potential bad runs, I would have missed all of the good ones, too.

---

5   Okay, it's more like a speed walk with a chance of running if my play-list shuffles to the right tune, but calling it *running* makes me feel, well, athletic.

I urge you to never stop running, whether that means literally or in some other area of your life. Envision your future and then run with it, believe it, and live it. Don't live your life based on limiting beliefs and don't let your present situation decide your future. Life is too short to stop taking chances based on your present circumstances. If you do, you could miss out on all the good runs. I urge you not to wait—those are the ones worth living for.

So there you have it.

I jumped into motherhood with no experience and quickly rose to become Mother-of-the-Year. I kept an immaculate house, had a three-course meal prepared by suppertime, and missed hours of sleep because of it. It was as if I had crossed over a hypnotizing, scarlet poppy field, altering me from being self-centered and egotistical into a groveling form of self-abnegation.

Living up to the standards I presumed my mother and mother-in-law were judging me upon left me feeling depleted, unhappy, and ornery. For me, it was the textbook recipe for burnout. And when pure exhaustion hit its peak, I *had* to implement self-care into my routine solely as a survival mechanism.

I now view self-care as a fuel for being a better mother, every day. While appearing selfish, it is actually unselfish, too. There is a difference between being self-centered and practicing self-care. And with straight-up trial and error, I found a balance between both worlds. I *could* take a half hour away from my kids and go for a run. I *could* put my laundry away first. I *could* paint my nails, but perhaps after a game of *Sorry!* with Weston.

Adding myself as a bullet point on my already daunting to-do list helped me immensely on my healing journey and raised my self-worth as a mom. And if my mother or mother-in-law had a problem with my new routine, at least Rachel Hollis would be proud of me.

CHAPTER THREE

In Quest of an Emerald City

By the time I had Weston, I had become a pro as a mother. Four years and two Dyson vacuums later, and I'm now a seasoned veteran, with stories that would make a new mother's blood run cold. But that experience has come at the cost of, well, *experience*.

Most of those experiences were nowhere close to Instagram-worthy, but they were full of unexpected comedic moments. I mean, how can you not laugh when the words "stop shooting your brother with your penis, it's not a gun" materialize out of your mouth?

My hair has been pulled, I have been peed on, and I have been yelled at. I can't tell you how many times my sanity has been saved by the five-second rule when a strong-willed toddler threw his brother's last cookie on the floor—and cookies aren't the only things that regularly hit the floor at meal time. I often wonder why I bother slaving over the stove for an hour when ninety percent of my efforts go to feeding the dogs—who have learned that if they gather around the table, they will soon be rewarded with a treat.

Our home has acquired its share of scars, too. There isn't a piece of floor in the house that the kids or the dogs haven't either peed or thrown up on. (Thank goodness for whoever invented stain remover and forgiving multi-coloured rugs. Hint: If I invite you over, I'd advise sitting on our couch, and not the floor.) You can actually tell the approximate current ages of my children by the height of the destruction on our walls. The older they've gotten, the higher the chipped paint and hand marks can be found. I often joke with Mike that we'll need a new house once the kids grow up because by the time they move out, this one will be destroyed.

That laissez-faire attitude was hard-won for my overachieving self, however.

For a few months after having Bentley, it seemed easy to present myself to the world as nothing less than spectacular, just as I used to do. Sure, I had to plan for an extra shirt in the bag in case Bentley spit up on me, that's no big deal, right?

But the shorter I got on sleep—especially after having to give up coffee temporarily—the things I used to pride myself on in my Mother-of-the-Year early days started disappearing. Then I lost the babies. And then Weston was added to the mix, dispelling the last vestiges of my perfectly ordered world.

By the time Bentley was five and Weston was two, the home-made buns were replaced by Costco specials. Even with best intentions, daily cardio sessions were sometimes taken over by daily runs to the laundry room (which have somehow not been enough to drop me back to my pre-pregnancy weight, despite the stretchy athletic leggings I regularly sport while doing it). I gave up on keeping my hair perfectly pinned and regularly turned the lights off during sex so my husband wouldn't see the rolls on my stomach.

Looking dishevelled most of the time made me feel as if I had failed, but I was too tired to do anything about it. I had spent most of my life preoccupied with my physical blemishes and shortcomings, but now I simply didn't have the energy to care. I threw my trophy in a closet somewhere behind the slim tailored red pants I used to wear and muttered "it is what it is" (my new survival mantra) for the hundredth time that week.

One day, I was going through an old photo album looking for a picture for Bentley's kindergarten "All about Me" project and came across one of my favourite photos of Bentley and me. While on a family vacation in Nova Scotia when he was about twelve months old, we came across a magical and secluded, sandy beach. It was the *perfect* afternoon—you know, the kind you take to the memory bank. Mike, Bentley, and I had built sandcastles and marvelled at the water teeming with starfish and other sea creatures we weren't used to seeing in the prairies. In the picture, I'm wearing a bikini and holding Bentley in front of me, trying to cover up my body.

I was the fittest I have ever been.

I'd die to be that fit again.[6]

Looking at that photo, it struck me that in every bathing suit photo I'd ever had taken, I was hiding behind someone else. If the camera came out, I'd angle my body behind the nearest solid object—my husband, my children, a picnic table, *anything*. If someone shorter than me was nearby (a rare occurrence), I'd grab them and pull them in front of me before smiling for the camera, all in an effort to hide those last ten pounds I could never seem to shake.

As I stared at the photo I realized something profound—those tummy rolls were where all of my life's most fun and spontaneous memories were harboured. That fluff around my middle held the long summer night hotdog roasts and s'mores around the campfire. That third roll underneath my boob—you know the one I'm talking about—was one too many glasses of wine with my girlfriends. Why

---

6   Well, not really. But you get what I'm saying, right?

on earth had I put so much energy into hiding my weight? The extra fluff carried the weight of unforgettable moments, too.

From that moment on, I determined to stop hiding my physical imperfections. It wasn't a failure to have missed my goal weight. Besides, I'd rather have those extra ten pounds of friendship and comradery than constantly turn down social engagements for fear of the extra pounds I'd have to lose afterwards. And I'd rather be present with my children in moments of fun than have them look back through the photo album and wonder if I was even there.

The next time we went to the beach, I rummaged around in the back of my closet and dug out the bikini I hadn't worn since Bentley's baby days (hiding far beneath that dusty trophy). When I tried it on and looked in the mirror, the flab was still there. I almost took it off—then I shrugged, grabbed the sand toys, and took my kids to the beach. And no one looked at my rolls twice, least of all my two boys. It was such a liberating feeling. I had wasted so many years trying to be perfect that I had often missed out on the spontaneous fun around me. I didn't want to waste another moment trying to impress the outside world. And I've got to tell you—I feel *complete* freedom now when I flaunt those tummy rolls.

I now hold the picture of Bentley and me close because it taught me to stop hiding my outward flaws. Who cares if I have messy hair or an extra roll or two? Trying to be perfect was an exhausting expedition and only made me feel more like a failure. Even when I got to my "perfect size" and had freshly made buns prepared for supper, I wasn't content. I still wanted more.

It was like being on a quest to find a City of Emeralds, made of green glass and other jewels, only to discover the entire city was a humbug creation. It wasn't made of emeralds and other fine gems, it was merely a city where everyone was made to wear green-tinted spectacles. The city was no greener than any other.§

That's when I let the idea of perfectionism go—I was human and I was never going to be perfect. That was my moment—that's when I made the final decision to walk past the Guardians of the gated wall of flawlessness and officially welcomed grace to join in.

The key to letting go of control, for me, was learning to live in the ebb and flow of every day. I released the illusion that everything needed to be in picture perfect order. Once I let go of my expectations—*poof!*—my disappointments floated away like a hot air balloon into the open sky.

Sometimes, your day might go like clockwork. And sometimes, you might miss a doctor's appointment or skip a workout. But guess what? The world doesn't end. "Whoops, can I reschedule?" has become of my favourite catchphrases.

There will be times when you forget it's Bring Your Favourite Toy to School Day, but there will also be times when you rock dinosaur birthday cupcakes for the classroom party. There will be times you'll show up to school in pyjama bottoms and with unwashed hair, but there will be times when you'll rock the parking lot in primed makeup and heels.

It's called balance.

And it's not just perfectionism in yourself you need to let go of. Your kids, are, well, *kids*. They are works in progress—very, very messy ones.

I have struggled with the fact that young children are naturally messy creatures. I despised finding fingerprints on my white bedding or water stains on my bathroom wall from a water gun fight in the bathtub. I resented coming into my bedroom in the afternoon to see my neatly made bed destroyed from a pillow fight.

I would shudder every time the kids would run from the table with their mouths covered in peanut butter, holding a glass of freshly poured milk sloshing in their hands. As soon as dinner was finished, they'd slide from their chair and run, and I'd yell after them "Please go wash your hands before you—!"

But those are the moments.

Those are the ones that mischievously slip past you without you even noticing. Time goes by too quickly. If you only worry about all the dreadful parts of your journey or focus on getting to the end, you might miss out on an incredible trip of discoveries to cherish along the way.

It's when you're surrounded by the complete and utter mess that you should be the most present and aware. And the secret to becoming present is to find the magic in the mess.

That doesn't mean every moment becomes magical. As I said in the previous chapter, it's not all roses. Some days my children challenge me more than others. There were times my babies cried until they broke me. I got frustrated with spilled sippy cups, vehicle crumbs, and unnecessary whining.

During the early baby years, I didn't enjoy the lack of sleep, my over-caffeinated bloodstream, or the lack of personal grooming. But there were so many other things which trumped the rough patches—the snuggles, the hugs, the family trips, the forts, the naps, the school field trips, the summer lake days, the camping nights, the slow walks, and the plethora of Kinder Eggs (which all good witches know have magical powers to soothe minor booboos).

Those everyday moments with my kids made some of the happiest memories I have. As time takes their baby years further away, the bad fades into a golden glow of good. *Who knew? All those other veteran moms were right.*

Several years ago, I began to share my parenting worries and faults in person and online. To combat Fear of Missing Out (FOMO) syndrome every time I opened up a social media app, I redefined "Instagram-worthy" to myself. Picture by picture and word by word, I displayed the truth. I stopped having fake conversations. I dropped every darn bit of the facade us millennials have been socially conditioned to present.

I deliberately chose to no longer spend unnecessary time and energy comparing myself to my friends, my neighbours, and my co-workers. I steered my car into my own lane, focusing only on my own family and our next best destination.

When I welcomed grace into my life, my guilt started to dissipate. Grace taught me to actively seek out the present moment, replacing FOMO with NOMO—the Necessity of Missing Out. NOMO changed my life.

For my own sanity, I started declining some invites and missing some non-essential appointments so I could fit everything in. If I was too tired to do something, I'd agree that doing the best I could was good enough. I'd extend the timeline of the task into the next day, chanting *tomorrow is another day* while doing it. Sometimes, I was busy doing nothing—recouping from our crazy with rest and relaxation became a requirement. Don't underestimate the vital importance of laying on the couch with nothing pressing to do for maintaining your mental equilibrium.

I bought sugar cookie kits instead of making cookies from scratch. That's right, Martha Stewart, I purchased the cookie kit from Walmart. The premade kits taste awful, but all of those small details don't really matter. You know what your kids care about? The quality of time you spend with them, not the quantity. So spend your time together on the fun parts, like icing cookies, instead of creating a big, old mess that will cause you a bunch of stress you don't need.

With all of my newfound life choices—NOMO, grace over guilt, and premade cookie kits—I became a *lot* happier. And so did my family.

Not long after Weston started sleeping through the night, I established the habit of waking up earlier than everyone else in my family. I found I needed that time to center myself and get ready for the day before the crazy zoo door opened for business. That extra hour in the morning allowed me to enjoy my coffee hot, without noise or distraction. If I fancied, it gave me the freedom to read, write, or even, on rare occasion, fit in a morning workout session.

I soon discovered the value of a morning routine: Get up. Make Coffee. Drink the coffee. Put on a bra.[7] Make the bed. Read, write, or work out.

And let it be known here, of all the gifts God gave the world, the one I'm most grateful for is coffee. Sure, I had to give it up for a bit, but I was eventually able to add it back onto my grocery list. Had it not been for that beautiful golden seed from the heavens above, I probably wouldn't have been able to function as well as I did during those early survival years of motherhood. And the best part is, no other mom judges you for drinking coffee when you have babies in the house. Cocaine, smoking, heavy drinking, maybe, but not coffee. They know what it's like trying to function on four hours

---

7   Probably the most important item on the list for increased productivity levels.

of sleep a night. Coffee is a wonderfully accepted drug of choice amongst the troops.

All of my morning rituals set the tone for the rest of the day and, like an iPhone battery (which needs recharging *all* of the time), if I practiced them faithfully, I felt recharged and ready to go each day. By the time little feet started pattering across my floor, I was ready to tackle the day that lay ahead of me.

At least, that's what would happen on an ideal day. But sometimes, an extra hour of sleep was necessary, and I missed those morning check-ins with myself, leaving me feeling "off" from the very start.

You know how it is—once those little babies get up, it's go time. In our house on the morning of a work day, we generally have an hour to eat breakfast, dress, brush teeth, and maybe even squeeze in TV time before it's time to get out of the door. The morning is often rushed and not an enjoyable experience for any of us.

I'm so glad the flies on the wall can't talk and remind me of all the times I've yelled the kids into the car. I would be angry at them because they had dragged their feet and yelling seemed to be the only thing that would motivate them, leaving them grumpy little Munchkins, too. As the adult, I realized that my reaction had contributed to their long faces, which made me feel even worse.

So I'd also do my best to turn the mood around (and lower my guilt) before leaving them.

"Who's ready for a great day?" I'd call over my shoulder.

If no one answered the first time, I'd say it louder. If only one set of hands went up, I'd say it even louder.

I'd turn on their favorite song and not stop asking until the rear-view mirror showed all four of those precious little arms up in the air waving like they just don't care. I set the intention that every day had the potential to be a great day before I left them, even if I was rushed and late for work.

If there's one thing I want to instill in my kids, it is this hard lesson I've learned: their attitude is one hundred percent their responsibility and no one else's. They can let a rushed morning ruin their day, or they can choose to turn it around, just like I can.

When I get up in the morning, I choose for it to be a great day. Even if my life isn't that exciting, I can still make it an amazing day, because my happiness is all about my own attitude, no matter what my life throws at me.

One December day in the throes of my healing journey, I went through a typical all-hands-on-deck morning to get the kids to daycare. I urged the boys into the car, then noticed the car seats were still in our truck from the weekend. I grabbed the seats from the truck to move them, grouching to myself over the fact that Mike hadn't moved the seats like he was supposed to. As I yanked open the car door to buckle in the first seat, an avalanche of fast food remnants came tumbling towards me, along with the most recent toy from McDonald's, some miscellaneous rocks, and a half-eaten waffle.

I stared at the mess around me and burst out laughing at the poetic irony.

Oh, my dear God! I've become the Cheerio Lady! Except I'm the Waffle Lady.

And to commemorate my new way of living as a Waffle Lady, last year for Mother's Day, I scheduled myself a photo shoot with my kids. I never have photos with *just* me and the kids. I'm always the one behind the camera, taking the photos. If, for some reason, I'm not able to see my kids reach their adolescent years, I want them to have a good picture of me as a young mother to keep as a memory in the years to come. No more hiding in the shadows. I decided to give them a picture of the Waffle Lady in action, revealing every imperfection and blemish I possessed—the wrinkles, the laugh lines, even the new grey hair which had made its shiny debut when I turned thirty.

I wanted to capture the reality of what our time together looked like—being constantly interrupted with Netflix video requests, building Lego, or receiving spontaneous bear hugs out of nowhere. And let's be honest, I wanted a piece of them, too. I wanted to remember the little cheeks I squeezed and the mischievous eyebrow lifts they used to give me. I wanted it all.

I'd give them evidence of the happiness they brought back to my life, a moment in time encapsulating all the things they had given to me as a new mother—gratefulness, presence, and perspective. My babies and all their wonderful joy and mess had filled my little Kansas farmhouse to the brim.

The kids and I raced to make it to the photo shoot on time with barely enough time to finish my curls or brush their teeth. I hadn't made the effort to buy nice shoes for the kids, so I decided we would take the photos in bare feet. *Good, that's more natural anyway.* At the last minute, I stuffed some photo props which made us, well, *us*, into my Matt & Nat bag: the closest coffee cup I could find, some toy cars, and the Lego pail.

We managed to get out of the house in one piece, and almost everyone had socks on. *Win for the team!*

The photographer captured all of it—all of our imperfections—perfectly.

Bentley's sweet, inquisitive, and perfectionist nature shone through in photos of him agonizing over the perfect Lego brick to use. (The poor kid didn't fall far from the tree.) She captured

Weston's goofy grins, firecracker temper, and big heart. (Like a bull in a china shop, but with a heart like gentle Ferdinand.)

While the photographer posed us for one of the last shots of the day, I remembered the middle-aged woman who had looked longingly into my cart of chaos at Walmart a few short years before. *That lady had it right.*

These were the days I'd one day long for. I needed my babies as much as they needed me. And it was at this photo shoot when I decided I wasn't going to miss another second of it.

I would no longer complain if I woke up in the middle of the night with a foot in my rib or a piece of Lego stuck to the middle of my back. Just like the indents in my flesh from a few misplaced toys, those first years—the sleepless ones, the thankless ones—are the ones that can indent and shape you the most. Life would be much less fulfilling without them.

The time of raising children is precious, but exhausting. Trust me when I tell you that letting go of control and perfection is a genuine survival mechanism during those early mommy years. Like a City of Emeralds, perfection doesn't exist, especially when you're raising babies. The photo shoot was a visual of the mother-lode of motherhood and the realities that come with it—as well as a reminder of the milestones my babies would soon be leaving behind. That's where all of the real jewels lie.

These days, Bentley is getting too big to have a bath with me. His legs are outgrowing his bed. His clothes keep getting smaller. He doesn't want to hold my hand or kiss me goodbye in front of his friends at school anymore.

Weston doesn't like it when I call him my baby—*Mom, don't call me that, I'm a big boy now.* He complains less when I leave him at daycare because he can understand why I'm going to work. He has intuitively started to colour within the lines. He's beginning to wipe his own bum.

All these moments remind me that too soon I'll be kissing my Munchkins goodbye along their own yellow brick roads. Which is why I must remember the magical mess that got us there.

I found complete enchantment in our mess when I implemented gratitude into my daily routine. Having gratitude for every good part of motherhood made me forget what wasn't perfect. I began to wake up each morning with more passion, intent, and purpose than I had the day before. I mentally slowed down with new appreciation for life itself, simply thanking the universe that I was healthy, alive, and breathing. I gave each day the potential to be the most beautiful day of my life.

Happiness came more easily when I started being grateful for all the problems I didn't have. I became grateful for the simple things which I used to take for granted, like access to education, power, and running water—some of those items aren't readily available in other countries. I became grateful that our family's basic needs of food, clothing, and shelter were always met—some people aren't as lucky. We often forget that one person's gratitude list might be someone else's wish list.

And the end of my day is no different. I choose to go to bed with gratitude. Every night, I set up my next morning for success by thanking the universe for every good part of my life.

Because I found it so useful for myself, I implemented a gratitude exercise into my kids' bedtime routine, too. I created a bedtime game called Three Things, keeping it simple and easy for them. I ask my little babies to tell me three things they liked about their day, and that's it. They genuinely love the game and remind me if we don't play it before I leave the room.

Even at their tender age, I'm teaching them to find the magic in the mess.

On your motherhood journey of finding magic along the yellow brick road, remember that the key to the treasures within is to celebrate the time for what it is. Things are messy and chaotic during the initial baby stage. It can even be really hard sometimes. Your house might be cluttered with items you don't really need, and your laundry basket might be overflowing and self-renewing, like mine. Your fitness regime might have to fly out of the door for a few months, or even years. But over time, you'll regain balance. And one day, you'll find yourself sitting around with some other veteran moms, laughing about the Great Poop Incident of 2014.[8]

In the meantime, make sure you take time out of your busyness to capture your present, even if you're in survival mode. Wear the darn bikini. Learn to be okay with the mess, the marks on the walls, and the chips in the paint. One day, your house will be clean and quiet, and you'll miss the noise, I promise.

Oh, and one last thing. The next time you come across another hot mess momma bear—you know, the one dressed in pyjamas with no makeup on at the grocery store—give her a high five and the benefit of the doubt. She might just need the extra smile and wave of encouragement that morning.

You never know—one day you might just turn into a Cheerio (or Waffle) Lady, too.

---

8   Mike still doesn't think this incident is funny . . . But I do . . .

CHAPTER FOUR

It's Not Easy Being Wicked

As Bentley transitioned from clinging to my legs to wanting to be just like Daddy, I watched my husband with envy. How could he handle our son's growing needs with such ease while, most of the time, I felt like an impostor still desperately hoping no one noticed I hadn't read the imaginary parenting manual?

Then I started noticing something else that concerned and bothered me—Bentley was not just emulating his father. He began to model some of my own mannerisms and speech patterns, but not necessarily the ones I'd hoped for. It started with a lack of confidence and fishing for compliments when I'd ask him to sing the alphabet, then escalated to him repeatedly hitting his head if his marker went out of the lines of his colouring project.

When I'd see him throw his beautiful Lego creation at the wall in anger because it wasn't perfect, I'd feel a hot rush of shame because I knew where he'd seen that modelled—in me. And that's when I made a deal with myself.

It was time for me to start colouring outside of the lines.

I was human. It was okay to make mistakes. It was okay to heal in front of others instead of hiding away in solitude, fear, and shame. I'd teach my kids how to possess an indomitable spirit by creating one for myself first.

I was bulimic, and it was time to heal.

I was only fourteen when I began wolfing down food and then purging to feel more in control of my life. The tipping point for me had been a comment made by a close relative the year prior. I was told I could never be as thin as my sister, Jennifer—my bone structure was simply bigger than hers. The simple, thoughtless comment spun me around like a cyclone picking me up from my safe, warm life and into a place of inferior status. (In reality, Jennifer and I weren't all that different in size. But the comment made me feel as though I were a giant beast and my sister was a dainty China girl found in the Magical Land of Oz. Reality didn't matter, only my perception of it.)

Even now, when I can look back and shake my head at the adult who should have known better, the words still sting. Every time I think of that moment, I'm right back in it, cowed by the finger pointed towards my face. I'm quite certain my relative had no idea they had struck my biggest trigger—comments about my weight. I didn't see it as their opinion, or even a statement of fact that was as unproblematic as the difference in our hair colour. I saw the comment as a directed criticism, like my weight and bone structure were an error in my being. It caused a childhood trauma and had lasting effects.

To this day, I actively have to turn off the knee-jerk negative reaction if someone makes a comment that involves both my sister and me. It's my relative's finger pointing out my flaws all over again. *Are they about to criticize me or are they simply trying to say something kind? Will I need to defend myself or should I thank them for their concern?*

That comment was not the only one I had ever received. Comments about my weight had been aimed at me since I was a little girl—I can remember receiving one as early as the age of six. For some reason, the moment I greeted extended family members, they felt it their duty to compare the weight differences between my sisters and me and how much my body had changed since I last saw them. Little wonder that those perpetual comparisons developed into an eating disorder.

It got to the point that when I'd enter a room full of family members, I'd stick close to the wall to try to avoid the dooming comment I knew would come my way if Aunt Em noticed me. Her, and my *very* honest grandmothers . . . I would avoid them like the plague. But sometimes I'd be caught off guard and a comment would come barreling at me without notice. I'd drop the cake that was about to enter my trembling lips and blink back the threatening tears.

As a child, I had no tools to cope with the way adults treated me or what they said about my body. I was raised to respect elders and didn't know if I was allowed to say something snooty in reply. So I did what I was taught. I smiled politely in response to their rude comment and walked away with a heavy heart. I began to hide food, indulging in private to avoid the comments I didn't want to hear. It's a habit I still have a hard time breaking, almost twenty years later.

As an adult looking back to those pivotal moments, I can now see the potent nature of words. Like magic spells, words have the power to cast positive, neutral, or negative consequences. Words have the ability to crack a person's confidence into shards. And even if that confidence can later be repaired, whether with glue or with gold, it is often with great difficulty, time, and cost. When a plate breaks, it will *never* be the same. A crack will always remain. So it is with people.

Might have I acquired an eating disorder had I not received countless negative remarks regarding my weight? Honestly, I don't know. I was young and I didn't possess the emotional maturity to properly deal with them. What I *do* know is that those openly expressed observations didn't help the matter.

The first time I heard the word *bulimia* was in my school health class. While the lesson was supposed to warn us of its unhealthy nature, that class did nothing but electrify me. My ears perked and I sat up straighter, intrigued with the new details I was hearing—*here* was the solution to losing the weight I couldn't seem to shed. A shortcut, if you will, for fitting into the size twenty-seven jeans my older sisters both wore.

Shortly after that class, I had my first binge and purge. We were eating a meal at my auntie's kitchen table, and the plate of garlic bread always seemed to end up in front of me. It smelled delicious, so I ate multiple pieces, nearly the entire loaf—not because I was hungry, but because it felt so good to chew and swallow those buttery pieces of warm bread. I wasn't sad, nor did I need comfort. I just ate because it felt good.

For me, a binge was not about hunger. It was *never* about hunger. It's about the need to feel good in the moment. I was comforted, full, and happy. But then the guilt set in. I stared at the empty bread plate and shifted beneath the tightness of my pants, thinking about how much the scale would condemn me the next time I stepped on it.

I contemplated what it would be like to not have the repercussions—the calories—of that binge. I thought about what they had said about bulimia in health class—about how to do it. Could I actually make myself throw up? *If I could eat what I want but not gain weight, I could become thin. Perhaps the unwanted comments might finally stop?*

At fourteen, I attempted bulimia to satisfy my curiosity. I quietly made my way to the bathroom, leaned forwards, and lifted the toilet seat. Staring into the unclean toilet bowl disgusted me, but not as much as the feeling of an overfull stomach. I closed my eyes, stuck my fingers in my mouth, and before I knew it, my experiment was complete. Then I cleaned up and made my way back to the table with no one the wiser.

Little did I know that this was only the first experience of what would become a habit that lasted into my late twenties. As the years passed, regular purges became a way for me to neutralize feelings of anger, to calm my anxiety, or simply to purge unwanted calories. I could eat ten cookies at one sitting without consequences. It was wonderful—or so I thought.

I was never caught, but the guilt and fear of being caught was ever-present. Before long, I became a pro at hiding my habit and maximizing my return.

I never left the table too soon, or I'd look conspicuous. I'd run the tap water or lock both the bedroom and bathroom door—hopefully giving me two entire rooms of empty space to avoid others hearing me retch. *Come on, I don't have much time.* I'd flush twice and wipe the tears out of my eyes, perhaps even brush my teeth, then return to family duties as though nothing had happened. If I was in a public washroom and someone disrupted my mission by walking in and sitting in the next stall, I'd have to pause and wait until they left the washroom to continue. *How annoying. Do you have to sit right next to me?*

I learned that the timing was important—it had to be not too long after eating and not too soon. If I didn't allow the food to settle, I would go through a period of fruitless and exhausting heaving, but nothing would come up. If I waited too long, the calories were in there for good, and then I had to deal with not only the guilt of the binge, but also the potential weight gain of an entire pizza. I knew I'd had a good session if I saw stars or felt dizzy after a purge—that meant *every* calorie had made its way out. Success was mine.

I'm not sure if anyone I saw after a purge knew what I had just done. But if I was in public, I didn't care. Wondering if I had thrown up all of the calories was the only thing consuming my mind. The only time I really tried to hide was around my immediate family—I knew better. I didn't want help, and I knew if they found out, they would make me stop somehow—*it* was mine, and I wasn't letting it go.

Purging was a way to escape my emotions when life seemed out of control. No longer did I have to feel disappointed when Mike called to say he was going to be late. I didn't have to feel angry when my plane was delayed, and I was two hours late getting home. I didn't have to feel anything if I didn't want to. I could eat cookies, tacos, and chips, and then I could purge the unwanted calories away. *Voila, I'm no longer angry or disappointed, I'm neutral.*

Due to how infrequent my purges were, I never thought of my eating disorder as a big issue. It was never an everyday thing, so I didn't consider myself a *true* bulimic. I simply took the disorder out on loan when I needed to shield an uncomfortable emotion or lose my last five pounds. (Spoken like a true addict.)

When I decided to become whole within, I knew it was time to deal with this issue at last. I was addicted to eating food instead of feeling emotions, but I couldn't keep doing that if I wanted to be a good parent. Regardless of the intensity of my eating disorder, the issues behind it needed to be tackled if I were to ever loosen the clutches of its grasp.

I wanted to be the best version of myself for my family. They were my *why*.

Now I needed a *how*.

I found hope in Gary Zukav's book, *The Seat of the Soul*. He suggests your addiction is the aspect of your personality that is most in need of healing, covering your greatest inadequacies. He states, "You cannot release the addiction until you understand the dynamic that underlies it. Beneath every addiction is the perception of power as external, as the ability to control and use the environment or others. Beneath every addiction is an issue of power."¶

The paragraph knocked me over when I read it.

Those were the dynamics of *my* situation. My eating disorder masked the actual problem—my need for control.

Even though I knew what I was doing was wrong, the tight grasp of my addiction and the illusion of power it gave me were too strong. In my early twenties, when I tried to stop purging on my own, I couldn't. I had nothing to replace the void with. The eating disorder itself was masking what I needed to heal the most—my need to communicate my emotions when I felt irritated, disappointed, or desolate.

I couldn't control what other people said about my weight. I couldn't control someone taking credit for my work. I couldn't control when Mike arrived home at nine o'clock after the kids were in bed and the household chores were done. But jamming my face full of sugary goodness and then purging the excess calories—those decisions were *mine*. (And I say that in a creepy, gremlin-like voice.)

I coveted the power I felt during those purges and left every episode feeling nothing but glorious satisfaction.

When I couldn't control what was happening around me, food could—it was as simple as that. Food helped me avoid feelings I didn't know how to handle. Food helped me curb the things I wanted to say out loud, but didn't have the courage to say. I finally saw that if I wanted to be free from my addiction to food and my illusion of power, I'd have to give up the need to control every situation that didn't go my way.

But, thanks to Zukav's book, I also realized I couldn't reach what was in front of me until I let go of what was behind me. I had to go out on a limb if I was ever going to reach the fruit. For me, that looked like pulling every comment about being overweight that had instigated my eating disorder to the surface. No matter how hard it was, I had to feel them, say them, and then let them go.

All of those comments and actions had been out of my control—but I could control my attitude towards the people who made them. I could stop giving those comments mental real estate or letting them define me. Moving on and releasing judgement was in my *complete* control. I could forgive every ignorant and unnecessary comment that had ever been made, purposely or not.

I wrote each comment onto a piece of paper and had a burning ceremony. I acknowledged them, I felt them, and then I let them go. The ashes rose and disappeared from view . . . and from my heart. I gave the world their heaviness so their weight could no longer hold me down.

After releasing my hurt, the next onion layer to be peeled back was my addiction to food. That was going to be difficult, because I loved any type of food. Over the years, I had learned to eat out of habit, not out of hunger.

Then I read about the Rat Park studies conducted at Simon Fraser University in British Columbia in the late seventies by psychologist Bruce K. Alexander and his colleagues. Alexander set out to prove that drugs did not cause addiction, which he believed was attributable to a person's environment and not to any addictive property of the drug itself.[9]

To test the hypothesis, the researchers built a spacious environment that came to be called "Rat Park" which was about 200 times the size of the standard laboratory cage. The Rat Park contained around twenty rats of both sexes, food, toys, and excess space for play—the perfect environment for a rat to thrive in. The other animals were housed in isolated environments in standard laboratory cages that held only the bare necessities.

In each environment, the rats could drink a fluid from one of two dispensers, one of which contained a sweetened morphine solution, and the other plain tap water. The rats living in Rat Park drank mostly from the plain water dispenser. The rats isolated in cages with only the bare necessities went for the dispenser laced with morphine.

In other words, rats relied less on the addictive drug when they had a supportive environment around them.**

I had an epiphany—being in control was my addiction and comfort food was my drug of choice. The solution to my problem was building my own Rat Park by upgrading my social support system and removing unhealthy food from my environment.

I began to educate myself on nutrition. If you consume more calories than you burn, then you'll gain weight. The math seems

---

9   The results of his experiment and acceptance by the medical community were complex, though did seem to somewhat support Alexander's findings.

ridiculously simple, but I had never actually done it before. For instance, I never clued in that the calories in a chocolate bar were seven times what you can burn in a thirty-minute walk. I always thought they were equals. *Large chocolate bar does not equal short walk, got it.*

Next, I upgraded my social environment. I surrounded myself with people who promoted healthy eating patterns. I stumbled upon a support group, finding a great deal of peace in talking about my feelings surrounding food. I worked through some of the distressing childhood comments that tormented me. I listened and felt supported when I expressed my thoughts, comforted in knowing others had food addictions, too. I was no longer alone.

The support group I met with became my weekly counseling session. I was encouraged to replace my unhealthy habits with healthy coping mechanisms. When I felt an anxiety attack coming on, I journaled, sat with my thoughts, made a cup of tea, or went for a walk. In ten minutes, the feeling would dissolve. The substitutes I found replaced food as my crutch, and my active eating disorder dissolved.

I learned to *sit* with my feelings rather than mask them with quick and swift dopamine hits like online shopping, excess eating, or caffeine. Real freedom came when I practiced feeling every emotion that came along with being human. And it was a bigger job than I ever could have anticipated—like trying to coax a cat to nap in a blow-up chair that's bobbing in a pool. However, even though changing old habits was uncomfortable and unpleasant, the result was miraculous and oh-so-worth it.

One of my favourite books to read to my kids was *The Color Monster* by Anna Llenas. In order to understand his mixed-up colours (which represent feelings), the Color Monster decides to sort them into jars. Blue is sad, yellow is happy, green is peaceful, and so on. Once he has all of his colours sorted out, he feels better.††

I enjoyed the book more than my kids did. For years, I had been the Colour Monster—my colours were all mixed up, but instead of sorting them, I'd become the Cookie Monster, sneaking cookies from the basement freezer and eating until I could no longer feel. Once I started identifying and sorting my emotions, I started to feel better.

I couldn't rewrite the last decade and a half of my life, but my story wasn't over yet. I had the power to alter the future by changing my attitude, perspective, and habits. I was ready to start a fresh new chapter.

Today, I would still classify myself as a recovering bulimic. I say *recovering* because triggers—in various shapes and sizes—will always present themselves. You don't stop cold turkey one day and wipe your hands clean of a once-treasured habit—at least I didn't, and seriously, kudos to those that can. Each day and each trigger are opportunities to choose healing, another step on the road to recovery.

No one wants to talk about eating disorders. When I started talking about my miscarriages, the reaction was usually empathy and warm hugs. In most cases, women I talked to wanted to tell their story about their own miscarriages. When you tell people you have an eating disorder, your audience looks towards the floor, not sure what to say. But I started talking about it because I know I'm not the only one.

I can see the signs of bulimia from a mile away—gobbling down food without enjoying it, tears in the eyes after excusing oneself too quickly from the dinner table, the smell of vomit in a public washroom or seeing someone's feet turned towards the toilet, and the small particles of food that remain in the bowl after flushing. You can't fool me—I'm a veteran at hiding the evidence myself.

Still, in my experience, no one wanted to talk about it. I've now shared my story countless times, but only three other people have ever confided in me with their own situation or experience. Just three. And even then, that's all that's said before the conversation moves briskly along. No sense lingering on the details, right?

My own confession didn't happen overnight—it wasn't easy admitting I had a bit of wickedness in me. Years ago, I gave my first, halting admission to Mike before we were married—the person I felt safest with. I had to let him know if he was to be *my one*. In my mind, if he accepted my most dreadful part, it meant he had the strength to love all of me and not just the best of me. After that, if a friend confided in me with a shaming secret, I'd sometimes let my confession slip out to let her know I didn't live in a glass City of Emeralds, either. *None of us do.* But it wasn't until I tackled it head-on that I realized how shame feeds shame—no one wants to talk about it, so no one talks about it even when they need to.

I never knew how much energy it took to hide my secret. For years, I had felt like a malevolent witch, safeguarding her most precious and prized possession while being consumed by shame because of it. But with each confession, the embarrassment around my past lost its mystical power. And each time I shared the truth, my voice grew less shaky and my confidence level rose. Like the Wicked Witch of the East when she had a Kansas farmhouse land on her, my intimate secret withered to dust, leaving behind a pair of glittery, enchanted heels—or in my case, an opportunity for a new chapter to begin.

I'll never forget the moment I owned my truth on a larger scale. I was with a large group of women—some new acquaintances and some old pals. When I introduced myself, for some reason, I kept talking and talking. Suddenly and without warning, my confession slipped out. *I love to bake, read the latest non-fiction release, and, oh, I'm a recovering bulimic. So, about that taco dip, what's the secret to the sauce?*

I surprised even myself when it popped out so naturally—it had been a well-guarded secret, one I was accustomed to hiding. Although awkward to bring up in an introduction of yourself, I apparently didn't feel the need to hide behind it any longer. I was flawed, like every other human on the planet, and I was apparently okay with admitting it at last. It was a part of my past that would always be attached to me, and I figured I might as well own it so I could move forward.

After that night, I didn't care who knew. I started talking about my eating disorder more freely. Recognizing and releasing the most debilitating part of my story made it easier to let go of other stories that weren't serving me. Owning my truth made room for the creation of new stories, but with much better content. And even better yet, I was now in a position to confidently choose how the rest of my story ended.

Brené Brown hits the nail on the head in her book, *Rising Strong,* teaching her audience *"not to deny the story, but to defy the ending— to rise strong, recognize our story, and rumble with the truth until we get to a place where we think,* Yes. This is what happened. This is my truth. And I will choose how this story ends."‡‡

Acknowledging what resides in your own onion layers will allow you to peel them away, too. So, give yourself the grace to change the ending of the story you no longer want to be attached to. Because when you do that, you get to choose how your story ends. You get to pick up the pen and write your own ending.

Want in on a little secret? There are days that I still stumble and fail. It's not often, but there have been times when I can't control the urge to binge and fall off the wagon. (I mean, *hello*, let's introduce a stressful global pandemic and take every remaining illusion of control away from me all at once. No wonder Dorothy felt disorientated when her whole life got turned upside-down by a coronavirus cyclone.)

But I try not to beat myself up about it. I remind myself that failing simply means I'm trying, and I haven't yet succeeded at my goal. I keep an imaginary button of forgiveness and grace for myself, and when I screw up, I press the button and start over. And there's no limit to how many times I can press that button.

Reset. Realign. Restart. Refocus. Reclaim.

And hold on to your *why*.

Once I found my why, I didn't have to have it all figured out to take the next natural step forward. That was enough. From that point on, I was ready for more.

My why, to this day, is raising my boys into gentlemen and good human beings. I didn't want them to grow up with the insecurities I had. I was determined for them to grow into confident, self-reliant men, which meant Mike and I would need to be strong examples for them to follow. I wanted them to know that mistakes are okay, and do-overs are a necessity.

Without my children, I would never have done the hard work of healing—it is a laborious and backbreaking job. But being a good mom, and a good example, to my children was worth the effort of battling with my internal struggles and bettering my soul.

Make no mistake, there is a reason why you were placed here on this earth at this exact moment, during this exact lifetime, surrounded by the environment you're in. I believe there is a rationale behind the pain you and I experience. The exact reasoning may be beyond your knowledge, as it is for me sometimes, but I guarantee it's getting you to a higher place than you were before. I believe healing our souls is the work we were brought here to do.

Whenever I'm going through a difficult patch in life, I often ask myself the purpose of the current pain I feel. *What if what I'm feeling is here to help complete my soul? What if it's igniting healing in all other areas of my life?* And I allow myself to feel the pain. I let it take space in my body, leaving me with more resilience for the next pain I have to go through, and then I release it back out into the world so I don't have to carry it alone.

So keep on living, breathing, and restoring. Heal the wounds you need to mend to ensure each breath you take continues to have purpose here on earth. Choose to be the beacon you were always meant to be. You are here to make a difference in someone's life— perhaps it's with a simple confession, like me. Maybe that one little thing you share and heal from will help someone else feel safe enough to begin their own healing journey.

That's what I hope this chapter does for someone, too. Maybe even for you.

CHAPTER FIVE

The Evolution of a Sawdust Heart

Before I had children, tangible gifts were very important to me. I associated gift-giving with love. The more material gifts I give, the more I love—has a ring to it, doesn't it? The problem was that I used that as almost my sole form of expressing love.

Instead of calling up a close friend on her birthday, I'd send a fifty-dollar gift card from her favourite store. Instead of going to visit a mom with her new baby, I'd send a virtual gift certificate for cleaning over email. I always had a good reason for this—I was too busy to call. Work needed a project completed. I had an appointment. The excuses could go on and on. The reasons were real, and I felt no guilt for this behaviour. Why should I? Giving gifts was my love language. After all, if the gift was something I would enjoy receiving, why wouldn't someone else?

Love and money were interchangeable goods to me, and I assumed everyone else thought that way, too. Just ask my sister, Jennifer—it annoyed her terribly. For years, she tried to explain to me that money did not equal love. In her opinion, performing selfless acts or giving things without monetary value equalled love—cleaning my grandma's windows because it was difficult for her or baking our dad cinnamon buns for Father's Day (his absolute favourite) were true gifts.

I didn't comprehend her definition of giving gifts until Mike and I had kids.

My definition of what a true gift entailed really began to change once the boys reached preschool age and started making crafts in art class. Their gifts to us spanned across the entire house—hand-painted crafts and drawings hung on our fridge, and jars filled with dandelion bouquets decorated the windowsill above our kitchen sink. Heart-shaped rocks and feathers found on our daily walks occupied my office space.

At the end of our day, Mike and I would crawl into bed to find Lego structures set on our bedside tables. It became a bit of a competition to see which one of us received a Lego structure or not. You see, our parenting behaviours were being skillfully judged by the boys daily, and if we weren't behaving quite as they thought we should, we went to bed with an empty nightstand.

The boys weren't the only ones teaching me what true gifts were either. Mike adapted the types of gifts he presented to me after we had kids, too. If I had a hard week juggling daycare drop-offs, school pick-ups in the middle of my workday and making it to hockey practice on time by myself, Mike would step in on the weekends. He'd wake up early on Saturday with the boys, allowing me to sleep in. I would take the rare opportunity to decompress and read a book by myself for the first two hours of the day while the smell of freshly made waffles and bacon permeated our bedroom. I'd take those mornings over a new pair of lustrous earrings or a bouquet of flowers any day.

He'd enter our bedroom with a steaming cup of coffee with one teaspoon of hot chocolate powder stirred in, just the way I liked it.

Without a word being spoken, he'd set it down beside me and make his way out of our room. As I watched him shut the door, the love inside that cup would fill me with warmth. Ah, a fresh cup of *hot* coffee—now *that* was a gift.

Receiving true gifts from my family drastically shifted my mentality around the art of giving. With each dandelion bouquet, detailed drawing, or bedside coffee delivery, my heart was rapidly changing in the most miraculous of ways.

The summer I met Mike, marriage and a family were the furthest things from my mind. I wasn't in the market to find someone to marry anytime soon, and neither was he. I had just turned twenty and was looking forward to working at a fly-in fishing camp in northern Saskatchewan for a few months before returning back to university. He had planned to go to Texas to custom combine—being a harvester for hire—for the next several months.

But the universe had a better plan than either of us could have ever imagined.

I had several friends who had worked at a particular fly-in fishing camp the previous year, and I had my heart set on doing the same. It sounded so romantic and glamorous—getting paid to work at a wilderness getaway far away from civilization, surrounded by fresh air and nature.

I went to interview after interview, but I was declined for all of the camps I applied for. My dreams of summer adventure were squashed. I needed some sort of an income, so I accepted a position as a retail associate at an agricultural outlet in the town I grew up in.

Inside, I was pouting. How was I going to have the adventure of a lifetime while sitting next to my mom watching the fourteenth season of *Survivor Fiji*?

When I complained to my mother about missing out, she replied, "All things happen for a reason. They always do. And one day, when you're least expecting it, you'll see it."

As it happened, the job Mike had gotten in Texas didn't start for two more months. In the meantime, he started working for his dad at the same agricultural outlet I had been hired at.

He had grown up in the same small town as me and we were only two years apart. But still, I really knew Mike by name only. His parents had divorced when he was eleven and he'd moved away in the sixth grade, long before my dating years began.

I fell in love with Mike over a cup of hot chocolate that summer. And when the time came for him to head south, he decided to stay. The rest, as they say, is history.

When we met, neither of us knew anything about life. We got married five years later with not much more on our life experience resumes. A year and a half later, we became parents—and unwittingly entered into a period of our lives I now refer to as the Years of Revolving Doors.

I'd walk out our front door in the morning with two kids and five bags in tow. At eight o'clock that night, Mike would waltz in the back door to brush the kids' teeth and put them to bed before finally eating his supper. On most days, we'd meet each other at the doorways with a head nod of acknowledgement, like two ships passing in the night. Sometimes, I confess, I'd completely ignore his presence out of resentment at having to parent all by myself all day yet again.

It wasn't fun parenting alone. Nor was the rat race of keeping up with our children's schedule. Between work, social and sports activities, supper, cleaning, homework, and sleeping, within five short years our life had become a cyclone—and not the kind that takes you to a magical land where you get a rocking pair of magical heels.[10]

No matter what anyone tells you, nothing can prepare you for the responsibilities that come with having a child. Parenting is an exhausting expedition that never truly ends. Those beautiful little souls are a full-time job from the moment they arrive. You're never paid for overtime, nor do you get any breaks between shifts. The income in relation to the number of inputted hours is unparalleled.[11] Oh, and the job never ends—you're needed for the rest of your life. If this is the Yellow Brick Road of parenthood, why is it such a strenuous, never-ending uphill climb? *Is there a fairy godmother I can call for this?*

As I mentioned earlier, because Bentley had been born three weeks early, he had spent the first few days of his life in an incubator in the NICU. When we finally did get to bring him home, I was overcautious with his every movement. I don't know if it was because of this or if it would have happened anyway, but my first few months as a new mom were an emotional roller coaster ride of epic proportions.

When Bentley was a few weeks old, we had some company over to see him. They were gushing and overjoyed. I was supposed to be happy and entertaining, but all I wanted to do was take a half-hour nap. My eyes were bloodshot and burning from lack of sleep, and me and my Type A personality were still coming to terms with our

---

10   Though we did see an awful lot of Munchkins during the never-ending playdates . . .

11   Or is it the other way around? I'm too tired to remember.

new—and non-existent—agenda. Overwhelmed and panicking, I took advantage of the fact there was another responsible adult in the house holding the baby and barricaded myself in the bathroom. With my cell phone, of course.

I didn't have a fairy godmother to call, so I called my sister, Jennifer.

"How can I continue to love this hard or protect this much for the rest of my life?" I said in barely audible whimpers. "Why didn't anyone warn me of the realities of parenting before I blindly jumped in? This is no joke. I could die with this little sleep!"

After thinking she may never have children of her own, God had answered Jennifer's prayers and sent two children her way—and she'd already been battle-scarred and toughened by their training regime. My novice snivels made her laugh.

"Do you think if we knew what we were in for as parents anyone would actually sign up for the job? It's the world's best-kept secret for keeping the population status on par."

I, of course, survived those first sleep-deprived weeks, and everything since. But nowadays, time to myself is still a luxury. It's something I must schedule if I'm to have any at all. Even if I get up early with the intention of tackling extra work, I'm never able to reap the full rewards of the sacrifice. Practically every time, Weston, our early riser, is sure to hear me and join in the fun. He's got that Mom's-up-so-I'm-up kind of attitude. It's just when I settle into my desk chair with a nice hot cup of coffee that I usually hear his looming shout, "Mom, I'm hungry!"

However, despite having the flying house of parenting land on me, I'd say the scene was pretty much a prerequisite in saving me from my wicked ego, along with so many other negative things. Over the last six years, my children were the ones to give me some of my most treasured gifts—adventure, new friends, wisdom, and strength to be who I wanted to be. I can't thank them enough.

Prior to that humbling flying house scene, I rarely had to venture out of my comfort zone. I was caught up in my own egotistical desires, worrying solely about myself and my life goals. I was busy climbing the corporate ladder and never appreciated slow walks with a loved one. You would have *never* caught me having an impromptu ice cream date with a child or even a friend—I counted calories, not memories. Once I had my children, my perspective on what really mattered changed.

I became flexible, learning how to place second—my way was no longer the *only* way. I learned how to gracefully lose arguments that didn't matter in the long run. I quickly figured out the benefits of evading an impending argument with a four-year-old. It's not worth it, trust me.[12] It just leads to a tantrum of epic proportions, which means no learning happens and no self-discipline is acquired. (And the kid isn't very happy, either.)

I became dexterous—and I mean that as literally as possible. I can now open a banana peel with my non-dominant hand and close a cupboard door with my foot, all while pouring milk into a cereal bowl. I didn't *have* to do all of those jobs at once before having children, so why would I? It's not the kind of thing you do just to see if you can. Well, some people might, but not this girl.

But over and above the gratitude I feel towards my children, I have to thank my husband. Mike was the partner I never knew I needed, but he was also the one who gave me my children in the

---

12 Well, except if you know the consequence will end up costing you, like allowing your four-year-old to not go to the bathroom before bed, and then having to wash the sheets in the middle of the night after an accident. That, my friend, is an argument worth pursuing . . .

first place. He is a man of true heart, compassion, and a steady work ethic. In fact, without him, I'd still be searching for my own heart.

I probably don't have to tell you that finding the person you're supposed to spend the rest of your life with can be a tedious and tricky process. Whether you want to admit it or not, I'm sure you have quirks and flaws a-plenty. And if you're lucky enough to find a partner who accepts all of those things about you, well, *that's* the kind of love to look for. You have to find someone who is willing to stretch and grow with you as the years go by. And you have to hope they'll accept you once you change, too—because, babe, if you're doing it right, you will.

In my opinion, the real trick to love, at any age, is to be all in. Not just in the Revolving Door Era. And once you find that perfect partner, the key is to never take their love for you for granted. Remember, they choose to be with you, just as much as you choose to be with them.

Now, I know I'm still a young pup and I have a lot to learn yet, but my brief experience spent between revolving doors—raising young children and not having enough time for myself, or my marriage—has helped me grow exponentially in the relationship department. It has given me the light to see that this period of revolving doors is when you need to be the most intentional about your relationship with your partner. It's the foundational base for the rest of your life with them. *No pressure, right?*

We had children at an early age, which meant we were still getting to know each other on a level of sleep that was simply unacceptable. We could have easily turned on each other, but in order to get through the baby years, we leaned on each other and parented together. We *needed* each other's strengths to survive. We knew those years had the potential to make or break our marriage.

We chose to let those years *make* our relationship. And we continue to let our hardships strengthen our relationship.

I believe you choose a partner who is the best fit to help you to heal from old wounds. You end up picking a person who complements the qualities you lack and who will give you tools to assist you in your own process of healing.

That's what my Mikey did for me.

In the short time we've been together, he's helped me heal from old and current emotional wounds by showing them to me in a different light. The patience and perseverance he taught me allowed me to parent better. He's made me stronger in so many ways. He's made me calmer and less reactive to situations I cannot control. He is so entangled into my very essence, I don't know how I would ever go about replacing someone so near and dear to my heart.

He's my "get to" person—he's the person I *get* to do things with, not *have* to do things with.

He's the person I get to grow up with.

He's the person I get to confide my secrets to.

He's the person I get to raise my kids with.

He's the person I get to build a life, a business, and a dream with.

He's my reasoning, my sounding board, my calm.

He's my home.

Becoming a parent with Mike has been, hands down, the most rewarding endeavour I have ever undertaken. But, as I mentioned earlier in the book, I wasn't exactly a natural. Mike, on the other hand, seemed born to look after babies. (My mother was thrilled, and relieved, to find out one of us had a clue as to what we were doing.) To be fair, he had practice from caring for his two younger siblings, apparently learning a thing or two along the way.

He was the one who taught me how to tip a bottle upwards while feeding to ensure the bubbles didn't give our babies tummy aches. He taught me how to hold a baby's chin and pat their little backs to burp them. He stood beside me and guided me as I changed my first diaper for Bentley through the armholes of an incubator.[13]

I took my new role very seriously, even though the amount of responsibilities now on my shoulders was somewhat overwhelming. Mike and I were now parents and, whether we liked it or not, we were going to leave imprints on these little humans. To some degree, the choices we made for them would go on to define and determine how they developed into young adults.

As a young mom, I didn't want to disappoint Mike with my incompetent skills and wondered what I could possibly bring to the table. I didn't know if I had absorbed enough life lessons to be able to have the powerful effect on them I felt they deserved. I owed my boys the world in return for the intangible gifts they had already given me.

I loved the idea of giving my little Munchkins courage, wisdom, compassion, and the ability to know their way home. I wanted them to have a strong foundational root system and a safe haven to grow up in. And when they were ready to leave our home, I wanted gentlemen to walk out of our front door. In my opinion, our job as parents was to ensure they could make it out in the world without us.

Now that I had a plan of intention, I had to find a way to execute it. I wished to expand their horizons and perspectives quicker than mine had been, expediting the process by the twenty years (give or take) it took me to learn these particular lessons. But how could I expand their horizons while they were still young children?

---

13 Of *course* I'd have to change my first diaper this way. Apparently even God needs a good laugh every once in a while.

Then I remembered one of the most life-changing moments of my own journey—the trip where I experienced my own smallness for the first time. The trip that broadened my perspective more than any other before it.

It was when I first visited New York City.

As a teenager and young adult, I had been scared to venture too far out of the nest. I've never lived further than a hundred-mile radius from where I was born. I mean, I was sixteen years old before I ever crossed a city street by myself, for goodness' sake.

Eventually, the greater world revealed itself through my own experiences of education, work, and travel. By the time Bentley was eighteen months old, I had already travelled extensively around the world for both business and pleasure. When Mike and I decided to start trying for Baby Number Two, I felt the need to knock one more trip off my bucket list—New York.

Because I already felt the guilt of leaving Bentley at daycare five days a week for work, I wanted to minimize my time away from him. I scheduled the flight to arrive in New York on a Friday evening and to return on Sunday morning, leaving me one full day in the Big Apple—assuming there were no delays.

With little time to spare, and much to experience, I made up a list of the top ten things I hoped to see and gave them to my tour guide and hostess—my cousin, Laura. I had some big-ticket items on there, like "see a Broadway show" but, considering the short timeline we had to work with, I would have been delighted if I had only experienced a ride in a New York taxi or ate a hot dog in Central Park. (Oh, the things that thrill me!)

As the plane descended toward the airstrip at LaGuardia, I was petrified with the idea of navigating through the New York City streets by myself. The city sprawled for miles outside my window.

It seemed so immense—big enough to swallow li'l ol' me, chew me up, and spit me out. Every horror story of muggings and terrorist attacks I'd ever heard of ran through my mind instead. I was a sweaty mess by the time we landed.

At the airport, I slung the small backpack—the only luggage I'd brought for the weekend—over my shoulder and stepped onto the closest city bus I could find, taking note that my destination—Grand Central Station—was the last stop.

Laura had made the trek sound easy, but I couldn't stop clutching the straps of my bag with white-knuckled fists and staring at the other passengers. *My God, what was she thinking, suggesting I take a city bus? Can the locals sense my fear? Cover your palms, they'll see you're weak and take your purse.* I puffed up my chest to seem as if I had the courage of a lioness, but felt nothing but fear inside.

When the bus finally stopped at Grand Central, I cautiously made my way onto the street and looked up at a sky punctuated by skyscrapers. *I'm here, New York.* I took a deep breath and held my purse a little closer. Crossing the street to get to Grand Central Station, surrounded by hundreds of locals, was *nothing* like the first city street I had crossed at sixteen. I trembled my way into the station trying to look and act like a New Yorker, scanning for a familiar face. *Ahhhh, there she is.* When I saw Laura's familiar features across the gate, my apprehension subsided into relief. I'd found my way there all by myself, and I hadn't been mugged once.

The first time I'd been to the city centre in Calgary, I'd found it overwhelming, what with the hustle and bustle of people, the skyscrapers, and the one-way streets. But nothing could have prepared me for the wonder and astonishment that awaited me in New York City.

It bedazzled me in the most intoxicating way—the lights, the people, the buzz, the nauseating smells. Even though I was exhausted from travel, we didn't waste a minute. We took the nearest means of transportation—the subway, *check!*—to Little Italy for a slice of authentic New York pizza. I saw familiar movie scenes in every street sign and fire escape stairway. I was fascinated by the horses waiting for their next carriage ride in Central Park. Calgary had nothing on this.

My tour hit my whole list. I was able to see a Broadway show (*Wicked! Check!*), the Statue of Liberty, and Little Italy. We even experienced a very memorable moment trying to locate the statue of the indomitable sled dog, Balto, in Central Park. With little time to spare, we topped off our mini-adventure with martinis in Manhattan.

Oddly enough, my favourite memory from that trip had nothing to do with my top ten list, but what happened while I was riding the subway. It was so mundane, yet so completely out of my little bubble of normal life. I sat there listening to numerous languages, surrounded by human beings of just as many cultures. In that moment, I felt very, very small. Although I had travelled extensively up to that point, there was so much I didn't know about the world yet—I had so many more places to see!

What a wonderful feeling it was to feel little! Expansion as a human being starts with an awareness of how much you don't know. By feeling exposed and vulnerable, I became a little bigger on the inside. That's the key to becoming big in the world, now isn't it? You become big by feeling little.

As I travelled home from my whirlwind trek, I recognized the advantage I'd give my children if I taught them the same lesson I had just learned. However, considering where my husband and I had decided to settle, imparting that lesson could be a challenge.

We had established our roots in a small town in close proximity to where we both grew up. There were only a few other families who spoke a language besides English or grew up with a different culture than our own. However, we lived not far from a small city—a small fraction of the size of New York City, but a city, nonetheless—so exposing our children to other cultures and languages would be difficult, but not impossible.

After my year of maternity leave with Weston, I was euphoric to learn of a francophone daycare centre only a few miles away in another little town. It seemed like a small step, but it was an opportunity to give the kids an eye-opening experience. Not only did it provide exceptional care, but exposing them to a second language would be an advantage they could use to achieve future success and broaden their horizons. As we left the centre after our initial visit, Mike and I exchanged triumphant glances. *We hit the jackpot.*

Although I was sad to leave them there to go to work, I also knew I was letting them go to get bigger. I wasn't always going to be a safety net for them and I had comfort in knowing I was at least giving them something greater in return. Our kids would soon be figuratively riding their first New York subway. One small step at a time, they were learning to feel little to get big at a young age.

As they grow, we will continue to try to provide them opportunities to expand their horizons beyond the small world of our family and town, whether through travel, new experiences, or meeting new people. Unlike their mom, when they get to their first platform at Grand Central Station, I want them to step forward boldly with the courage of a lion.

And in my opinion, they are already well on their way.

When I was growing up, my dad would pack our lunches, and nearly every day, he'd include a Red Delicious apple. I'd open my lunch sack each noon hour and be disappointed because of that apple.

Now, to be fair to my parents, when I was a little kid, the varieties of apples available on Canadian shelves were limited compared to what's accessible in today's market—you could buy either a Red Delicious or a Macintosh variety. But it still didn't change the fact I'd have to eat that darn apple before I could go out for recess. I know, First World problems here, but there is a point to my story.

Once I left home, I had to shop for my own groceries. When I came across the apple bin, I gazed in astonishment at all of the varieties—there were apples in that bin that I never knew existed. Hesitantly, I picked a variety that looked appealing to me—a colourful, crunchy Gala—and put it in my cart.

I had finally found a keeper. I loved it and bought it exclusively for years until I ventured out of my bubble and tried a new one—the Jazz apple. Apples are now a staple food in my house and a go-to snack. My kids run around before bed time snack singing "an apple a day keeps the doctor away."

One day when Bentley was small, I was in the process of reading him a children's alphabet book and found myself stuck on the Letter A page. The page was filled with all sorts of apples—from yellow to red to green. I was brought back to the moment of opening my lunch sack all those years ago. Even within the limited market availability, I wished I would have had more opportunities to try more than one kind of apple.

I knew I wanted to give my children the ability to choose their own apple—in other words, have the aptitude to make their own decisions. I didn't want them to be as mindless as a scarecrow by the time they were sixteen, like me. To do so, I'd ensure they were exposed to as many different things as I could think of, so they'd know what appealed to them. And when the time came for them to choose their way in life, my hope was to give them the freedom to do so. (One can try, right?) My ambition is to respect whatever they end up choosing with no strings attached. I want to allow my children the space to be who they need to be.

I have so many friends who have chosen particular professions simply to impress or fulfill their parents' ambitions. We all want our children to succeed, but is fulfilling your desires a lifetime imposition you want to impart? Most of those friends I mentioned ended up being not very happy because they were living someone else's dream.

In my opinion, it's our responsibility as parents to guide, teach, and shape. I want to encourage our children to pursue passion in their work, instead of basing their decision on a projected annual salary outcome. My goal as a parent is to ensure my kids are happy first and successful second. I want them to find joy in waking up every day, working in a profession they'd essentially do for free if they had the option.

My next and probably most important job as a parent, is to then nudge over a bit and get out of their way. I have to let them go and make their own mistakes. Mike and I can support them without approving of everything they do, provided their endeavours are positive ones.

In his TED Talk "Do Schools Kill Creativity", Sir Ken Robinson tells the story of a problem child who simply couldn't sit still at her desk during class, fidgeting constantly and lacking any sort of focus. To the school system in the thirties, it appeared she was underperforming and seemed to have a learning disorder.§§

What happened next is *incredible*.

At the school's suggestion, the mother set up an appointment with a doctor. But the doctor saw something in the child the school did not. He left the child behind closed doors and took her mother to another room, but before he left, he turned on the radio.

And the girl started to dance.

The doctor told the mother the girl wasn't sick, she was a dancer—she had to move to think. Instead of medicating her child, the mother followed the doctor's suggestion and signed her daughter up for dance classes. The dance skills the girl acquired went on to give her immense fame and fortune in New York City.

The little girl in this story was Gillian Lynne, who is now a multimillionaire, best known for her work on Broadway hits such as *Cats* and *Phantom of the Opera*.¶¶

Through aptitude and wisdom, Gillian's mother epitomizes giving her child the gift of choice. When it comes to my kids, I hope to do the same.

With Mike's inconsistent hours, we never really know when he'll be home from work. It could be five o'clock or it could be nine o'clock—it all depends on trucking lineups and whether or not there are any breakdowns. As the evening approaches, you can find me on constant lookout from inside our front bay window, yearning to see him pull into the driveway. By then, I'm often starting to feel the fatigue of the day, single parenting, and a lack of adult conversation. Frankly, I'm desperate for help with the kids.

When I peer out to see him parked in our driveway, I exhale in heartfelt relief. When he walks in the door, the kids' demands of me will be cut by fifty percent. Instead of hearing the word *mom* ten times over the next ten minutes, I might be able to sit down for half a second and just breathe. *It's nearly time for my mental break.*

I impatiently watch him sit in his parked truck as he shifts his headset to the dashboard and shuffles his paperwork around. As much as I need him, I know he needs those five minutes to recover from his work day, too. His only time with us has to be squeezed into the next two hours before the kids' bedtime, leaving him with little time for himself. He knows the moment he walks through those doors, two rambunctious kids will be running and screaming with excitement to meet him. *Dad's finally home!* Two large huskies will come to rub up against him. He will have a list of requests from me.

As he walks towards the house, he usually has his head down, scrutinizing the challenges he has just faced. He doesn't know I see him sigh before he takes his first step up the stairs into our home.

But I do.

And the next part of the story is what amazes me most about my husband, because it's one of his very best attributes. When that man walks into our front door, his voice is cheerful, and he is wearing a huge smile. He is ready with open arms to catch the stampeding children running down the hallway to hug him.

You'd never know what had taken place beyond our closed door during his walk into our home. Mike chooses to leave behind all of his worries the moment he touches our doorknob.

It's one of the things I love most about him. But it's far from the only thing.

Mike has a knack for knowing how to pause in moments of crisis or how to let small fights go. When my knees hit the ground and I'm crying inconsolably, he's figuring out a solution to our problems, quietly and with ease. His ego has always been on the back burner—he's never needed to prove his worth to anyone by acclimating to the popular group. Since I've known him, he's always been okay with being himself.

Mike has the ability to give his best self to those he loves the most, even if he doesn't feel one hundred percent like doing it.

The man is like a fairy-tale Tin Woodman—embodying strong work ethic, great bravery, and patience beyond means. He is a man of true heart. And that's what I want for my boys. I want them to follow in Mikey's footsteps and learn to leave their troubles at the doorknob of any threshold they enter.

I want the boys to grow into compassionate human beings, like their dad.

Since I've experienced what receiving *true* gifts can feel like, I no longer appreciate monetary gifts, flowers, or jewelry the way I used to—they've all lost their old appeal and value. Having a cup of coffee set out in the morning made just how I like it or simply having the dishwasher unloaded can send me into a flurry of heated passion. Receiving little painted handprints in a smudged heart shape or a traced footprint crafted into an animal with construction paper and glue—*those* are the things that make my heart flutter.

Those are the moments worth counting and the gifts worth receiving. Those particular gifts leave me with a desire to parent right.

So, what Jennifer was trying to tell me about giving gifts was true—I told you she was like a fairy godmother. It just took a few jars of dandelion bouquets for me to figure it out. A true gift is one that changes your heart and leaves you wanting to be a better person. And when you are on the giving side, the truest gift you can give someone is a piece of your heart, with no expectation of anything in return.

I didn't know how much my sawdust heart could evolve before all three of my men entered my life. My heart's advancement in shape and size no longer left me craving cheap, plastic trophies scattered across my office desk to prove my self-worth. My trophies had been replaced with something much more precious—Lego castles on my bedside table. And those modest gifts left me knowing I had the best job in the world—being a mom.

It took becoming a mother to learn how I could channel the intangible gifts of courage, wisdom, and compassion to my children. But of all the gifts I could bestow, the greatest one I could leave to my family was my whole heart, with no expectations in return. Like any good mother tries to do, I could become the heart of their home. And there's no better gift in the world, now is there.

CHAPTER SIX

"Excuse Me, Where Should I Put the Flying Monkeys?"

When our kids started going to preschool, our family life felt like one tent short of a full-blown circus. Mike and I were happy to leave the baby stage behind us, but this new stage of life wasn't any easier—our lives became fuller, ballooning into gargantuan proportions. Between juggling work and our family life, I often felt like the Ringmistress.

New itineraries arrived without notice. Hockey schedules, school fundraisers, field trips, and birthday party invites appeared in my email inbox on a daily basis. I could no longer *just* go to work, I had to make my day job revolve around the kids' social life, school hours, and extracurricular activities. *And I thought dragging babies, lugging bags, and driving through winter storms on icy roads to daycare was challenging.*

Mike's unpredictable work schedule meant he could rarely help out with school pickup or running the kids to early hockey practices. On most mornings, he would leave the house before the kids and I even woke up, returning home only after supper was served and bath time was in progress. Some nights, we weren't even *that* lucky.

With raising the kids, working a nearly full-time job out of my home, and bookkeeping for our trucking business on the weekend, our marriage was put on the back burner. Focusing on invoicing a client in the middle of the night with a four-year-old on my lap became an average day at the office. There was no energy or time to focus on the other adult in the house. *Fend for yourself, there's leftovers in the fridge.*

Our life resembled a dazzling Ring of Fire—beautiful, but if you lose concentration for a moment you can end up in the hospital. And as time went on, it became obvious that the circus was on the verge of collapse. Something would need to change.

Trying to do it all showed me that I *couldn't* do it all.

Each morning, the circus begins with the same rushed routine— eat breakfast, brush teeth, get dressed, make beds. If the kids hurry, they're usually able to fit in a quick cartoon show. For me to make it back to the house on time for work, sometimes their remaining breakfast has to be set on their laps for the ride to school and daycare.

Since our kids are still at the age where they need assistance to get into the car and safely buckled, loading up can be a hurdle in itself. Between the school backpacks, ski pants, blankets, teddy bears, and water bottles, I often resemble a waddling clown as I maneuver through the garage, squeezing past the bikes and strollers while trying to avoid rubbing against the dirty car door.

Once I drop myself into the driver's seat, the kids usually hear a sigh of relief.

Under the big top—a.k.a. the daily routine, where I feel the most pressure—I often drop a few juggling balls between acts. When I forget indispensable items, such as a favourite blankie left stranded in the entrance or something even more essential, like keys to the car, it means only one thing—another five minutes on the clock, which I may or may not be able to afford to lose.

Once everyone is buckled and teddy bears are tucked in, I adjust the tunes and back out of the driveway feeling like I've already run a marathon—but, in reality, it's more like the first hurdle.

Our first stop is always Weston's daycare.

Once parked, I never know what kind of reaction I'll receive once I take him out of the car. He *could* nonchalantly walk into the centre himself or he *could* begin weeping, clinging to my legs for dear life. Mommy guilt *always* ensues with the latter. It takes me a minimum of ten minutes—and colouring at least one picture with him—before he agrees to stay.

Our daycare providers assure me he is perfectly fine once I leave, following up with a laughing comment about him pursuing a career in acting. Even if what they say is true, I never think the comments are funny—my heart aches to leave him like that, every time. *Am I a terrible mom choosing to go to work instead of staying at home during these precious years? Does he feel abandoned after I leave? Is he happily playing and colouring with the other kids or sitting in the corner pouting?*

During the next ten-minute drive to Bentley's school in the neighbouring town, I'm tormented by the image of Weston's sweet, inconsolable face and the guilt of actually *wanting* to go to work. I know the tension will sit with me for the next eight hours, and I can only hope to have thought-intensive projects to distract me. But first I have to cross the next hurdle—getting Bentley to school.

Upon arrival, I never try to rush him out of the car, because I know I'll one day miss those slow walks. With each school drop-off, I lose a little piece of him to his own independence. Still, I can't help but murmur to myself as we walk at turtle speed to his classroom door. *Are kids purposely slow at this age?* I try to hide my mounting panic that I'll be reprimanded for being late for my first conference call, *again.*

Once Bentley has safely settled in, I make my way out of the school, slithering past the hordes of children in the school hallways, trying to avoid as many people as I can—especially the parents of his classmates or, worse yet, his teacher. I don't want any of them to notice I haven't had time to wash my hair in days. *Thank goodness hats are acceptable garments . . .*

I'll be honest with you, on most days, I'm a hot couture mess when I step inside Bentley's school. I'm usually wearing the same leggings I wore to bed the night before. By the way, sweatshirt season is my favorite season—winter has the potential to last up to six months here in the middle of Saskatchewan and sweatshirts have the ability to hide all sorts of evidence. *Am I wearing the same t-shirt I wore yesterday? Maybe. Am I wearing a bra? You'll never know . . .*

As I rush back to my home office, I jump over the last hurdle of the morning, lunging into my desk chair as the clock changes to eight-thirty. Making it to work on time feels as if I've just conquered Mount Everest. Thank goodness I now work from home and my coworkers cannot smell the results of my herculean feat. (A little boob sweat never hurt anyone, amiright?)

I take stock of myself while pouring my third cup of coffee, and am thankful if the only thing on backwards are my pants. Luckily, Skype meetings only display my image from the torso up. No one can ever see my slippers beneath the desktop . . . I hope.

Over the past few years of working from a home office, I conjured a way to dress up for a meeting in mere seconds. Prior to any conference call session, I adorn myself with items from my secret office stash sitting beside my desk—an infinity scarf, mascara, lip gloss, and a pair of shiny earrings. *Business on the top, party slippers on the bottom. Don't forget to pinch your cheeks . . .* That simple pinch indicates shift two of *my* day is about to begin.

I blow out another long exhale and switch mental gears for a different kind of stress and pressure, pushing my mommy guilt to the background. Even though I appreciate my work of sifting through Excel spreadsheets to provide support to sales teams on the ground, my entire work day is a surge of activity I have to complete to get back to the thing I want to do most—seeing my kids.

It's the most peculiar feeling.

I've just hurried them all morning so I can get to my desk on time, and now that I'm here, I miss them terribly, counting the hours until I can pick them up. The exact moment I switch into work mode is the same moment I start to daydream about which book they'll choose to read before bedtime or which Three Things they'll choose to list as the best part of their day. In the thick of a challenging work day, I'd switch my corporate hat for my mommy hat in a heartbeat.

The closer the clock hands inch to quarter to four, the more the stress in my neck loosens. As I begin to close down my open programs, email inbox, and shut off my computer screens, endorphins rush into my system. The pressures of the office can stay at my desk and wait for me until tomorrow. All I can feel now is excitement that I'll soon have my little Munchkins with me again.

As I start up my car engine to pick up the kids, shift three of my day begins. *This* shift is the most enjoyable for me—I know the rest of the day is ours. I'll have the evening to spend with my kids, either at home or chauffeuring them around to their activities.

But through all of the shifts, I feel constant strain. The stress of each day works itself into my back, neck, and forehead. Each guilt-ridden morning drop-off leaves me questioning if I should leave my day job while my kids are still small. Perhaps it's the conundrum of every working mom—wanting to contribute and be an economic benefit to the family but feeling guilt for every moment not spent investing their time into their children.

It's in those moments I wonder if all of the rushing is really worth it. *What if this is my only chance to be with them? What if after they leave home they never* want *to return home? Should I really be pursuing a career at all?*

So many mothers have offered their points of view on what is best for my kids, my family, and our situation (whether I wanted the extra dose of guilt or not). In my experience, I found women's opinions to be heavily weighted on the side they've landed on— strictly being a homemaker, pursuing a career outside of the home, or somewhere in-between. Unsurprisingly, it was easier to talk to moms on my side of the wall—I received less judgement.

The working mom vs. stay-at-home mom debate was a conversational battleground I tried to avoid at all cost. *Heaven forbid I say the wrong thing and hit a landmine.* But it was easier wished for than done—snide comments about my decision to work sometimes found their way in from other women who stayed at home to raise their children. Sometimes, I was the one making those nasty judgements, too. We were all just trying to defend our own choices. Men, on the other hand, didn't touch the subject with a ten-foot pole. (Paternity leaves were just coming into play when I stayed at home with my own kids.)

One day, I found myself captivated, reading another mom's article titled *Should Mothers Have Careers?* It soon became obvious from her words that her answer was a resounding *no*.

That woman's words left me the most guilt-ridden I had ever felt.

It was if she had interviewed me for the column—all of my insecurities about working had been laid out before me, hooking me by the heart and pulling me into its whirlpool of guilt. I leaned into the article, perching at the edge of my seat as I read her justifications for staying at home to raise her kids. The words displayed there in black and white held the authority of facts, and I found myself nodding in agreement.

But later, I had to wonder if she had even bothered trying to see if the reverse were true. Had she ever walked in the shoes of a working mom? *Probably not.* She might not have been so judgemental had she bore witness to the other side herself.

The statements she made about the negative effects of being a working mom and the positive effects of staying at home with your children were all true. I had witnessed every point on her list in my own kids. But I also knew it wasn't the whole story. I had stood on both sides of the battlefield at some point, and I valued both lifestyles for different reasons—both had their struggles and benefits.

I loved my gig as a stay-at-home mom. My two maternity leave years with my kids were incredible. Tiring, yes, but incredible.

For the first years of their lives, I had my children and they had me. I could recharge from a sleepless night with a quick snuggle and nap alongside them. The laundry could wait—there was always time to finish it later. And when I finally got to it, the laundry was folded and put away on the same day it was washed.

The household duties were part of my job, and I took pride in taking care of my home. I enjoyed cleaning because I could do all of the daily household chores at a leisurely pace. I never had to rush to scrub a toilet or clean a bathroom faucet before making it to hockey practice on time.

I also had time to prepare dinners from scratch, including fresh homemade buns from an afternoon of baking. There were homemade dessert options at most meals. *Would you like a piece of fresh chocolate cake or chocolate chip cookies? Oh, hang on, I have chocolate pie, too.*

And to complete my Homemaker-of-the-Year application, I was even able to dip into my entrepreneurial side to explore my interests, opening up a home-based cupcake business.

When I stayed at home with my kids, I had the time and energy to be Super Mom.

I also loved my stint as a working mom—in fact, I still do. Going to work is like a holiday away from home. (Even though I work in a home office. Weird, right?) I enjoy having a hot cup of coffee undisturbed at my desk. Instead of a constant barrage of questions interrupting any and every thought, the requests that come my way are politely preceded with a "Do you have the time to chat?"

When I go to work, I get a break from the fighting, the whining, and the screaming. Someone else takes over some of the bum wiping duties. Going to work gives me a break from the mental and physical strains of motherhood.

When I stayed at home with the kids, my coffee usually had to be reheated three times before I took the first sip—that's if I could find where I'd left it in the first place. I was constantly interrupted with requests for snacks.[14] And I sometimes heard "Mom, can I"

---

14   Oh, good lord, the snack requests. You'd think I starve my children based on the number of times they ask for snacks during a twenty-four hour period.

so many times in a day that it started to sound like one word—
Momcanai have a cookie, pwease?

I was fulfilled at work in a different way than when I stayed
at home with my kids, too. My mind was challenged in different ways, and my projects were praised across the company, filling
me with a sense of accomplishment. Nobody was praising me at
home—soothing a baby in the middle of the night was a thankless
job—and, might I add, one that didn't pay very well.

Not only did I feel purpose at work, I was also proud of myself
that if something were to happen to Mike or our relationship—
heaven forbid—I could financially support myself and the kids.

There is something to be said for having individual economic
freedom. I can't count how many conversations I've had with other
women worried about leaving their husbands because they couldn't
afford the financial responsibility of leaving. They didn't have a
viable choice. I didn't want that for myself. (I'm not planning to
leave my husband, but I think it's reassuring to both him and me
that the reason we're together isn't because I can't afford to walk
away. Mike has often told me he's comforted in knowing he doesn't
hold one hundred percent of the financial responsibility of our
household, too.)

And earning my own wage gave me freedom to spend money
on anything I desired. I didn't need permission or feel guilt when
I'd shopped for luxuries or non-necessities. We've never had to go
without and neither have our kids. I took pleasure in treating my
family to a winter holiday someplace hot or buying new winter
boots instead of thrift store finds. (Seriously, the good ones can be
a line item on the budget on their own, and it's hard to get away
with less in a Saskatchewan prairie winter.) My rewards for working
mommy guilt were treating us to some luxuries in life.

I wish I could list *all* of the benefits my kids are receiving from me being a working mom, but I'm not far enough along to know yet. My kids are still young—we've barely escaped out of the baby and toddler stage. Mike and I have yet to climb the strenuous mountainside into their adolescent years.[15]

What I *do* know is that we all make choices for our own family situations and, when it comes down to it, those choices are none of anyone else's business. It doesn't matter if you decide to work, stay at home with your kids, or simply drop off your kids at daycare on occasion to enjoy a hair appointment with a Starbucks specialty coffee in hand by yourself. When you're doing what's best for you, you're ultimately doing what's best for your entire family. *Boom.*

I think it's clear to any of us that whether moms have jobs or not, *all* moms are working moms, and each situation is affected by its own unique challenges. Stay-at-home moms rarely receive the validation they so desperately need and definitely deserve as often as they should. And fellow working momma bears have to balance the pressures of an office environment with trying to maintain a household in some semblance of order in only twenty-four hours a day.

We're all in this together—or we should be. We as moms should support and uplift each other, whichever side of the column of we fall under. And if you find yourself judging the other side, perhaps stop and ask why. If I dig deep enough to the root of the issue, I often find my outer judgements are really just mirror images of my own internal struggles.

---

15 But when I do get to the top and you see me sliding down the other side with a cocktail in hand, I'll jot down some notes for you and put them into my next book.

Regardless of the benefits of having a career of my own or not, as I read that article, I recognized that doing it all, or *trying* to do it all, was taking a toll on me, my family, and my marriage. Before my maternity leave with Weston and while I was still commuting to an office, there was no time to relax. Weekends existed only to catch up on the necessities of life we hadn't been able to squeeze in during the week—laundry, housework, and picking up the groceries.

The circus was out of control, and there were winged monkeys climbing all over the guy-wires. *Just to confirm, those things shouldn't be here, right?* I was a complete mess, standing up on the high-wire on a unicycle with a dog named Toto sitting on my head, hoping to get from one end of the week to the other without falling off or falling apart. I was in survival mode. *Breathe, keep driving, make supper, read storybook, and then bed. Oh, glorious bed. I can do this.*

Our kids had made sacrifices, too. When I decided to go back to work, they had to learn how to be away from Mommy for a long part of their day. My job required some travel away from home—whether I liked it or not, it was still a part of the gig. I've spent countless days and weeks away from my kids due to work travel—*more than I'd like to admit to.* In the world of business travelling, it was classified as minimal, but I always felt guilty until the moment I came home.

My kids didn't get to relax in their pyjamas with a bowl of cereal and watch cartoons for a full hour before they headed to school like I had done as a child. They learned to hustle at the ripe age of twelve months. Their wishes were not always my command—I got to them on the weekend or in the evenings after work. My job often took precedence over their own plans.

And meals—the ones containing all of the food groups—had become a rarity. Fast food items like chicken nuggets became a staple in my freezer and a go-to in a pinch. My kids can spot the big yellow M from miles away, and the drive-in staff practically have our order memorized.

Me: Two happy meals. One hamburger, one nugget. Two white milks and the apple slices, please. Oh, and don't forget to pack the *boy* toy, I don't need a fight in the back seat.

Voice on loudspeaker: Oh, hi, Ms. Chelack. Tell the boys their dinner is coming right up.

Bring it on, McDonald's. Bring. It. On.

But along with the hustle, the time apart, and the dry bowl of Cheerios they sometimes ate in the car on the way to school, my boys were served a heaping helping of independence, social skills, and resourcefulness. When you can't run to Mommy the moment your friend disagrees with you, you learn how to handle it yourself. I was teaching them how to ride their own unicycle safely while I was learning how to stay on mine, too.

Still, the guilt remained.

Tired of quick foods and leftovers, one morning I got up early to prepare a complete meal with the help of the slow cooker. We settled in for supper that evening with the table set to celebrate the momentous occasion—a meal containing all of the food groups with dessert for the finale.

Bentley climbed up on his chair and stared at his full place setting—complete with napkin—with amazement. "Is this what a real meal looks like?"

I felt like I'd been sucker-punched.

As we ate that wonderful family meal, I knew I absolutely had to change something. Something had to fall off the table if I were to continue to work, parent, and do them both well. I could no longer try to do *all* of the things.

Bentley's comment on the rarity of eating a real meal startled me into questioning the viability of letting our situation continue as it was. Yes, I loved that we had nice things and went on extravagant adventures, but were we really happy with the shape of our lives?

When we went to the park, I looked like a clown car act. Picture this: Two large husky dogs securely tethered to my waist while I push a stroller filled with a toddler, snacks, and outgoing invoices. You could often hear me guiding[16] the biking child beside me to look out for the oncoming vehicle across the street. On the way, the mail got picked up and an extra jug of milk got purchased for a nighttime cereal snack, so I could check those errands off the list.

The dogs were happy, getting their daily run at the dog park. The kids were happy, getting a bike ride and park date with Mom.

Everyone was happy—except *me*. I hated feeling rushed, untidy, awkward, and sweaty on those walks. I hated that if I bumped into anyone I knew I was often ornery and out of sorts and only wanted to continue my walk through town without being noticed. But I also recognized that was *how* I got all the things done—by letting myself drop off the bottom of the list.

That's when I began asking myself, *how did it get this bad in the first place? I never signed up to be a clown.*

Before having kids, I never thought Mike nor I would have to take time away from work to care for our children. (Remember how naive I said I was when I became a mom?) Nor did I think I would become the main care provider in our home. I assumed Mike and I would be equals, like every other aspect of our marriage. As equals, I believed we would both contribute the same amount of time and energy when it came to our children—the perfect proportion of

---

16   Yelling at

parent to child, along with an executive-level membership at Costco and a rewards card at Home Depot.

I stared at the three-ring circus our lives had become, and it was apparent that one of us would have to step back from our careers to keep up with the new schedule. We had no other choice—the house of cards we had constructed was about to collapse.

It was time to hang up the clown suit.

Sacrificing our family's happiness for one week in Hawaii every winter didn't quite seem worth it anymore—the stress of our lives would kill us before we got to enjoy the promised relaxation. I sometimes joked about Mike having a heart attack at a young age over our lifestyle choices, but it had begun to not be funny.

I didn't want the repercussions of *doing it all* anymore.

The solution to our problem was learning *not* to do it all—at least, not all at the same time. I wondered, what if instead of hustling to build a life that *looked* good, we slowed down and cultivated a life that *felt* good?

And I liked the sound of that. But now the question was, *how do we do that?*

When I'd returned to work after having Bentley, I had worked full-time at the office in the city. After my maternity leave with Weston drew to a close and we knew we needed to take more hands-on steps to balance the circus act of motherhood, I was kindly granted a reduced work schedule from full-time to sixty percent and began working from a home office.

When it came to who should consider a reduced work schedule to be able to stay at home with the kids more, the difference in our salaries came into sharp focus—Mike was making more money than me. And he was more heavily involved in our business—he was the only dispatcher and drove one of the trucks. If he stayed home more, our business model would have had to drastically change.

It wasn't impossible for that choice to work, but it made more sense for Mike to continue to work full-time while I took a sabbatical from pursuing my own career aspirations. And I gladly took the lead on the home front, taking a time, pay, and position cut so our lives could revolve around school hours, field trips, and extracurricular activities. I was excited to take a "holiday" away from my career goals.

Within a year of returning to work and getting more sleep under my belt, I found balance and once again wanted to take on more. I was graciously granted my request of going back up to an eighty percent schedule, leaving me with Fridays off. That one free day still gave me a chance to catch my breath between acts. It left me time to fit in appointments and the ability to keep up with our general household duties. In other words, it kept me sane.

When Thursday evening rolled around, I could safely stow away my clown suit and red nose until the following Monday. On Fridays, the kids and I could casually sleep in, eat breakfast, drink coffee, and walk to school in a leisurely manner. Weston and I could wear our pyjamas all day if we really wanted to.

I loved my new lifestyle—at first. But then, like a parasite too small to see, resentment found its way into my heart.

Working at eighty percent was still a balancing act. Instead of a high wire, I was now walking on a plank while strapped into a safety harness, and even though it was bearable, it was exhausting. You can bet your booty, hockey practice on Thursday evening was served with a side of French fries at the rink to finish up our week—this momma bear was tired.

Our family life thrived because of my choice, but there were downsides. My professional life felt stagnant. I was bitter over the career path I walked further away from—my capabilities were far more advanced than what I had come back to. I stewed on the opportunities I'd let slip by when colleagues I had once interviewed and hired surpassed my pay grade and position level.

Meanwhile, friends and neighbours assumed I was *just* at home. I was once even asked if I could set up an after-school program at my home. I was at home, wasn't I? It was difficult to make outsiders understand I had an unconventional and flexible job, but I still had to report to a manager between the hours of eight-thirty and four.

I grew resentful towards my husband, too. Mike's career with our trucking business flourished because of my choice to step down in my own career. Yes, the company's success was for us, but I was the one holding up the pole in the middle of the circus tent. And I'd be lying if I didn't say my wage was also enabling us to subsidize the costs of new buildings, equipment purchases, and land invest-ments for our trucking business—so heaven forbid I complain about that. It was also funding us with the extras in life—holidays, health benefits, and non-necessity luxuries.

My choice to stop climbing the corporate ladder while con-tinuing to work was an incredible investment for us as a family unit, but I felt sour about my own career choices.

One day, I was briefing (which sounds more professional than saying I was whining, so let me have this one) a friend on my dis-appointments in my choice of career move—or lack thereof—when she stopped me in my egotistical tracks with, "I don't know what to say to you, Shari. If you don't like it, then quit."

I was slapped in the face with the cold, hard truth. I pulled up my chin and took a deep breath, adjusting myself in my chair.

She was right.

The way I was reacting was unreasonable and childish. I had made every limiting career choice up to that point, hadn't I? I was the one who chose to take the step back to help raise our family—no one else had made that choice for me. I had actually jumped at the opportunity when it arose. I was *excited* to break away from the day-to-day madness.

Mike hadn't even hinted that's what I should do—he would have supported my decision either way. I had been offered career leaps that would have required us to move to a different province, away from extended family, and I *gladly* chose to turn them down, even when Mike offered to move for me.

And becoming a full-time, stay-at-home parent was in my complete control. If I didn't want to be juggling every part of my life, I could quit the circus act of motherhood in an instant. We could learn how to live on Mike's wage alone. *When you make less, you spend less, right?*

So what was stopping me from fixing the issue of feeling daily resentment about my life?

A wise neighbour also accurately captured the motivation behind my choice to continue working, asking me, "Is it a matter of putting food on your table, or is it a matter of having a nice table to set your food on?"

That was it. I was embarrassed to admit she had hit the nail on the head.

I wasn't working to provide us with just the necessities of life, but so we could acquire the extras. Yes, I wanted a great health benefit package and savings plan, but that wasn't all. I also wanted to feel stimulated while earning a stable wage and contributing to our household disposable income. I enjoyed eating off of a nice table and didn't want to give it up. Ironically enough, the same choice left me with little time to prepare meals or actually use the piece of furniture I so badly wanted.

The conversations with both my friend and neighbour made me realize how ignorant and clouded my thoughts really were. I had *chosen* not to do it all, but I resented the fact that in order to gain the rewards of my choice, there would be things I would have to sacrifice. I was being offered plate service at the Ritz-Carlton instead of an all-you-can-eat buffet at the Go For Sushi joint and complaining about the price tag. Something had to fall off the nice table we were eating on—my ego—to make room for the elaborately prepared meal being presented to me.

That's when I remembered the life-changing lesson I learned three years earlier at a women's agricultural conference I attended.

The speaker had been drilling the importance of having a business card when a woman from the audience of six hundred stood up and meekly asked, "What if you don't have a job description? I'm only a stay-at-home mom who helps on the farm."

"You don't need a job title to define who you are and your value," said the speaker. "A business card is only paper, and you don't need someone else to tell you what should be on it. You need to take responsibility for your own worth."

Then the speaker told all the audience members to order business cards with nothing other than their name on it to hand out to new moms at school or anyone in need of their contact information.

I was floored. Before that moment, I had always assumed you needed a job to carry a business card. I assumed you needed a job title to be a *somebody*. This new idea of defining my own worth blew my mind.

As soon as I arrived home, I ordered cards with only my name and the title I wanted to define me beneath it. A salesperson came to my door shortly afterwards and, to hurry her away, I gave her my new card with every intention of screening her imminent call.

"Creative Lead," she read from the card, noticeably impressed. "What do you do for a living?"

I pointed at the card like it should be obvious. "I'm the creative lead in my life."

The simple creation of that business card allowed me to become the director of my own life. Starting in that moment, a job no longer defined who I was.

Three years after attending that conference, I finally took that a step further when I decided to own the choices I'd made to step back from my original career plans for the sake of my family. I'd claimed my place in the battlefield of life. It was now time to own that position, too.

I began to water my own grass instead of gazing across the fence. When I listed what I was receiving rather than what was being taken away from me by my choices, I found I was getting considerably more out of my new work schedule than I had allowed myself to see. *I was being given the gosh-darn opportunity of a lifetime.*

Filled with an immense amount of gratitude, I turned my attitude around from that moment on. I thanked my lucky stars, every single day, for what I'd been given—time with my babies. The two steps I had taken back in my career were giving me five steps forward with my family.

I was also gaining other benefits from my career choices. With a position in support, I was learning how to listen and follow rather than give direction. And once I owned the decisions that got me to where I was, I was finally able let go of the internal power struggle I had for climbing corporate ladders. I focused on myself, learning how to fight right and how to communicate properly—a completely new skill set, too. *Who cares if I'm right and they're wrong? It's four o'clock and I have more important things to do . . .*

I began to look at all of my choices as short-term. It wouldn't always have to be this way if I didn't want it to be. *Seriously, I could be dead in five years anyway.* Nothing was set in stone, and I could be a boss babe someday in the future when my babies didn't need me so much. In the meantime, I'd simply have to be okay with *accepting* my reduced work schedule, requested pay cut, and theatrical clown workshops first.

I *could* have it all, just not all at the same time.

I had finally figured out the key to my own success. I had wasted so much time and energy on pretending that I didn't have kids while at work, trying not to become the parents I used to judge when I first joined the corporate environment. I had acted like I was at the top of my game while running on four hours of sleep, just like I'd once expected those office parents to do. *Seriously, who did I think I was?*

Apparently, both Weston and I could have taken up acting careers—I mean, you totally buy that I actually *wanted* three cups of coffee in the morning instead of needing a stimulant to feel semi-cognizant for my eight-thirty meeting, right?

When my ego fell off the table, I stopped apologizing for having kids and working at the same time. I was now a mom first and an employee second. Work would no longer get the best piece of me—a good portion, sure, but only after my family had taken their piece of the pie. I'd even sliver out a piece for myself before work received their slice. Choosing to no longer apologize for living in both worlds gave me the opportunity to have a decent relationship with my children, probably saved my marriage, and definitely returned me to a sanity level I could live with.

To make the idea work, I needed compromise from both sides of my world. There were going to be some days that Weston would have to go to daycare when he didn't want to. I was going to have to miss a field trip or two for Bentley. I wouldn't always make it to afternoon school concerts, but I'd always make it to the evening ones. I'd try my best, using the eighty-twenty rule as a guideline—if I made it to eighty percent of their activities, I wouldn't feel so bad missing the rest of the twenty percent while I was away with work.

But there were things I *wouldn't* compromise for my family anymore. I was going to have to leave work early sometimes and make up the time after hours. I was going to have to take some conference calls on the road while on the way to school pickup. I might even have to have a sick kid on my lap while I calculated a formula or two on a spreadsheet. And if my workplace couldn't live with my new boundaries, I'd have to leave.

Similar to Shauna Niequist in *Present Over Perfect*, I'd aim at disappointing the people I cared about most—my family—as little as possible. Within reason, I'd slowly learn to be more and more comfortable with disappointing the people outside of that predetermined circle. I'd give anyone outside of my immediate circle realistic expectations of what I could and could not continue to do.***

I was a working, juggling momma bear riding around on a unicycle, and it was the circus act I could live with—I might just have to look a little dishevelled along the way. Apparently, I was a happier individual with flying monkeys swooping around me in intricately coordinated patterns through a circus tent. Learning to swoop, balance, and sturdy myself, was just the survival part of the game.

Even if my thoughts sometimes waver, which they do, deep down I *know* I've made the correct career and family choices for those around me that really matter. When I look back as an eighty-year-old woman, I will never regret the decision to be more present with my kids when I had the opportunity to do so.

The truth of it is, you're the creator of your own circus. And if you don't love the lineup you're a part of, you can change it. Or at least find a balance between both worlds, like I did.

No matter whether you're in a situation where you have to work to put food on the table and a roof over your family's head or you're working to supply a few extras, know there is always one thing you can control—your perspective. Instead of complaining about the work you do, choose to have an attitude of gratitude. Be grateful for your health and the skills that enable you to earn a living. Be grateful for the support you're able to give to your family. Be grateful for your co-workers from whom you learn so much, even if it's how you *don't* want to be.

Owning your circus and realizing you're the Ringmistress of your life will give you the power and choice to know when you *can* do it all and when you don't have to, or shouldn't. All good jugglers know you can't juggle all of the time—sometimes, you have to put your balls away in order to recharge.

And learn from the company of performers you live with—your children are the best teachers for showing you how to become a certified acrobat yourself. They will teach you how to use your limbs in ways you never thought possible. They will teach you how to use your time more wisely. And you will love harder and stronger than you ever thought possible.

If I hadn't been challenged to do it all—and then learn how *not* to do it all—I wouldn't have become the mother I am today. Declaring that my kids were more important than my work healed something in me I didn't know needed healing.

And if I made it out of the circus tent alive and relatively unscathed, I guarantee you can, too.

CHAPTER SEVEN

Confronting the Not-So-Wonderful Humbug Within

Bentley is our social butterfly and as he got older, it wasn't uncommon for one of his friends to knock on our door and ask him to come out and play. And any time he went outside, at least five other kids would join him. With approximately twenty kids under the age of ten on our street, he never lacked the opportunity to make a friend or two.

You would think this would be a good thing—perhaps even magnificent—but I'd watch him through our window, securely concealed behind a closed curtain and numb with fear. *Does this mean I have to be friends with the mothers of these children?*

Houston, we have a problem.

Making new friends terrified me. The small circle of friends I had was carry-over from my childhood. Due to a friendship that ended abruptly in my teenage years, I had blocked the ability to create lasting friendships since high school. In fact, I thought I was *unable* to make new friendships—and I was okay with that. I was perfectly content with the idea of becoming an old, lonely woman, crocheting with a cat next to me while watching *The Golden Girls* reruns.

Once again, the mere act of becoming a mother was bringing to the surface parts of me I didn't want to confront. But if I let the story in my head continue, I wasn't the only one who would suffer—my children's future friendships would be on the line, too. Because of undealt-with teenage emotional wounds, I didn't want my fear of developing friendships to imprint on my kids and stand in the way of them making friends. I might be okay with spending my life peeking at the world through the curtains, but I would not let that be my children's story.

That meant my introverted self would have to clean house on one more limiting belief, no matter how uncomfortable it made me feel. My kids had friends to make, and I wasn't going to get in their way.

Okay, kiddos, I'm doing this for you. Challenge accepted.

The limiting belief all started when I was sixteen.

My high school best friend and I did everything together—until, out of nowhere, she ended our friendship. She no longer answered my calls, and we no longer spent our weekends together. She ignored me in the hallways. I didn't know what had happened. To this day, I still have no idea why that friendship abruptly died.

In a graduating class of ten people, you can imagine the limited choices I was left with. I moved on with life, but the excitement was gone, like the clock had struck midnight and the party was over with only a broken mirror ball and some sad-looking glitter on the ground to show for it. I made some new friends and continued to go to the same weekend parties as my ex-bestie. We were civil enough to exchange pleasantries, but that was as far as it went.

I was *deeply* hurt by her rejection. And that's when the story in my head began.

Her dismissal left me believing I was not worthy of good friendships, or *any* relationship, for that matter. My pitiful story became a movie reel in my head, replaying over and over. *I'm not worthy, I'm not worthy, I'm not worthy.* What began as a story I told myself became an active fear in my everyday life for years after and, eventually, my reality.

Every relationship thereafter was affected by my thought pattern. I barricaded a safe area around me, essentially hanging a Do Not Enter sign around my neck. No, I didn't speak the words, but my energy pushed others away. Afraid of being abandoned or misled again, I became inaccessible to the outside world and was terrified of befriending anyone at all.

In university, I never made a single lasting friendship. As soon as someone became a smidgen too close, I would push them away. I only allowed familiar people around me, never venturing far outside of the bubble I grew up in for fear of bursting it completely.

And don't even get me started on how I felt about dating. I mean, c'mon. How was I supposed to meet someone new when I was afraid to allow anyone to get close?

Instead, I became the matchmaker amongst my friends. When someone asked for my number, I convinced them my friend was a more suitable option than I was. I dubbed myself Cupid, setting up numerous couples while not becoming involved with anyone myself.

It was the perfect solution for me. Guy was happy, friend was happy, I was happy. *We all win.* I could go home to solitude with a side of deep-fried wings, which was the way I liked it. I'd usually call Laura (yes, the same Laura who would later be my tour guide through New York City) to tell her I got home safely and proceed to fall asleep on the couch.

My thoughts had become actions and my actions had become habits. The habits I had created at the age of sixteen carried on for the next fifteen years of my lonely reality. Like the impostor con man of a wizard who created a throne of green and a giant head to run the country of Oz, the story of rejection I told myself came to dominate every part of my life, and I never questioned it. In fact, though I met Mike the summer after my second year of university, I wasn't exactly an easy catch—he certainly had his work cut out for him to get through my barriers.

My extended family saw how much I liked him and couldn't understand my hesitance in dating him. They jokingly referred to him as A Friend from the Male Species, and when he offered to make our relationship official, they insisted I accept. If I hadn't bowed to the pressure from my family, instead of being happily married, Mike would probably have been one more war story in a long list of Woeful Tales of Missed Opportunities I now tell.

So, you can imagine my aversion to Bentley's new craving for playdates—which meant not only the friend coming over, but also the friend's mom. We'd await the arrival of our new guests with completely different states of mind—him with excitement, me with almost paralyzing social anxiety. While making the coffee, I'd obsessively play out the potential scenarios in my mind so I'd be prepared to react like a *normal* mom no matter what came up. As Bentley bounced up and down at the window, excitedly pointing out the people coming up the walk, my palms would slick with sweat and I'd check the table one more time. *Coffee, cream, sugar, check. Let's do this.*

Once the child would walk in the door, the kids would run off to play. *Mom, bring us snacks and keep your new friend busy while we play with cars, okay?* I would stand there and give the other mom a plastic smile, wondering how on earth I'd get through the next hour and a half. I'd nervously pour coffee and try to make small talk, somehow making it through with my dignity mostly intact. *What if she finds out I'm a fraud?*

The most peculiar thing happened after a few of those uncomfortable visits, I started to enjoy the company. My feelings of discomfort turned into feelings of ease as our conversation would go on naturally with things we had in common. We could relate on some levels—these other moms had their own issues, too.

The coffee dates soon escalated into lunch dates. With my anxiety in overdrive, I went all-out on chicken curry the first time and watched the kids play with their food while the other mom and I made awkward excuses for our children's behaviour. The next time, instead of trying to impress the mom, I served chicken nuggets and fries shaped like happy faces—now *that* was a fan favourite. Most moms will agree that if you satisfy their little bundle of joy, it's an automatic win for you. *Whew, I figured out how to win at lunch hostess for toddlers.*

I sat through a few such visits before I noticed another problem that was developing—once I'd invited a mom and her child over, we'd often get a return invitation.

With the movie reel playing on repeat in my head, I spent every visit wondering what on earth these moms found interesting in *me*. *You want to meet again next week? Are you sure?* Not only did I like these women, it seemed they liked me too. For real. *That can't be right. I'm a weirdo. A weirdo people don't like.*

After it became obvious that they weren't just being polite for the sake of our children, I finally began questioning my lonely story.

What if the movie reel is corrupt—what if there is nothing wrong with me at all? What if I wasted fifteen years on my version of the story? What if the end of the relationship with my best friend had nothing to do with me? What if it was about her choices and I was simply collateral damage?

I never did ask her why our friendship ended. Honestly, it was high school and stuff like that happens. I didn't have the emotional maturity or confidence I have now. At sixteen, I could barely navigate a city street by myself, let alone the mires and crags of teenage relationships. The same was probably true for her.

Eventually, she did try to make it right. Over the years, she has sent apologies, invites, and even baby gifts. But I accepted none of them, hindered by my bitterness. I was still too angry and the more I clung to the story, the more debilitating it became. It was easier to believe the lie than work through the pain that caused it.

Perhaps the ending of our friendship was on her, but the rest of it—the healing from it—*that* was on me. I was both the creator and limiter in my own life—the sky wasn't the limit, I was, and the stories I'd created about myself. The limitations I was experiencing in my relationships as an adult were because of the choices I had been making since I was sixteen—but if I had made the choice to put up those limitations, I could also make the choice to take them down.

When I realized this truth, I began to look at the old movie reel through a new lens. I stopped blaming her for what she had done and became accountable for the last decade and a half *I* had wasted, not her. Now was my chance to stop the repeating scene in my head for good—choosing not to heal was no longer an option. I wasn't going to waste another moment on that story—my kids had friends to make.

I didn't know it then, but letting go of that story was the key to opening the door to living my authentic self.

I could make friends—the playdate moms proved that. And if I could make friends, then I must be okay. I was a weirdo, but I was a weirdo people liked. Having friends felt good—I no longer had to feel lonely all the time. Perhaps I could be like Dorothy, one of the gang,[17] and not the Wicked Witch of the West, looking in with an ornery cat and ball of wool on my lap. And, while I was at it, I figured I might as well attract people like me.

I turned on my weirdo light, letting it shine brightly so other weirdos like me could find their way. I talked about things I was actually interested in—meditation, psychic readings, and seeing signs from Spirit like feathers, number sequences, and hearts. (I know, talk about weird.) But I stopped caring about the response I'd potentially receive in return.

The most surprising thing happened when I started to share my interests and my abilities to read Spirit. The most unsuspecting of characters—older relatives, respected colleagues, and neighbours I had barely known before—came out of the closet with similar interests and abilities. *Who woulda thought?*

There was a significant lesson I took out of the entire experience: When you get hurt, you have two options on how you choose to move forward—you can *blame* the situation or the person, or you can *learn* from it. Choosing to blame is no different than continuing to carry the bricks from your past. Nothing changes and you end up building the same Yellow Brick Road. But choosing to learn, now that's the catalyst to transformation. In my case, I chose to learn something from the relationship that had tainted my perspective. I figured out how to belong among others again.

---

17   In both Oz and *The Golden Girls*. I'd be fine with either one.

The experience confirmed to me that all human actions, at their deepest level, are motivated by either love or fear. And most people cope by projecting their fears and insecurities onto others. Once I figured that out, I decided not to take anything other people said or did to me personally ever again. More often than not, when others lash out or hurt you, you were just in the wrong place at the wrong time. I took on the perspective that maybe what others say and do to you is never really about you, after all.

Shortly after deciding to embark on this monumental undertaking—you know, of making friends—I celebrated the bachelorette party of the salt to my pepper, Laura. We were born one month apart, so I believe that gave us an immediate bond—well, that, and the fact that our mothers are sisters. When we were younger, we had acted more like sisters than cousins, which wasn't uncommon behavior for my mother's side of the family.

My mother's side of the family had always had a close family bond, something I came to understand was uncommon once I saw how other families operated. Whenever there was a family event, *everyone* would come—*where one goes, the rest will follow.* And there were many such occasions.

So it was of no surprise to me when Laura's bachelorette party unfolded like any other family event. Some of my cousins flew in to make sure they didn't miss the occasion. Even a few of our uncles showed up alongside all of the female cousins and aunties.

In true family fashion, the party was one for the history books. We met at a local club to dance the night away. Every time another unexpected guest showed up, Laura would cry happy tears and her soon-to-be-husband, Mike (I know, *another* Mike) would look amazed at the close-knit clan he was marrying into. Our group closed down the bar, two-stepping and singing karaoke to old, familiar country songs. As we all went to settle into our hotel beds for the night, we promised to meet for breakfast for one last hurrah before everyone's flights started leaving.

A few hours later, feeling a little worse for wear, I sat quietly at our table at Denny's, holding my coffee mug and observing the other occupants. Even in my morning misery, I recognized how incredibly lucky I was to be sitting there surrounded by my family, some of whom I saw far less than I'd like.

And then it hit me—I had been searching for something I already had.

All this time, I had pined for close friendships, but I was never really lacking—I had just been too consumed in my own debilitating story to see it. Without warning, the curtain I'd been using to protect myself was ripped away, exposing the fraudulent, humbug rejection lie I'd been telling myself for fifteen years. I could stop believing the booming voice in my mind that told me I was unlovable and couldn't make friends—I was not alone. And I'd *never* been alone.

I'd always been surrounded by loving relationships and people who understood me. I had family that would drop everything to come to a bachelorette party or be there in your time of need, and a cousin I considered close enough to call a sister. They accepted me for who I was—just like I did for them.

Sure, our group was a little mismatched—more like the ragtag group accompanying Dorothy to the Emerald City than the similarly clad Munchkins who sent them on their way—but the trusted support system I had yearned for was always there. We were mismatched *and* united. Now that's a friendship!

I was surrounded by connections who possessed courage, wisdom, and kindness, staring at the small, sad wizard who had deceived me. And now that the lie had been revealed, I, too, could safely come out from behind the figurative curtain I had spent so much time trying to conceal myself behind.

I'd been searching for Instagram popularity, trying to live up to an impossible picture-perfect standard to be liked while being afraid of making real-life connections. But I finally knew that's not what I needed. It was better to be accepted by a smaller group who loves you as you are than to be accepted by a larger one filled with strangers who expect you to be perfect, or worse yet, like one of them.

As I laughed with my extended family around that Denny's table, I understood that the things we yearn for can often be found close to home. Realizing I had always belonged gave me hope. Now, I could safely add to my existing circle. I could take down the electric fence and Do Not Enter sign and finally allow people in.

It didn't happen overnight, though. Out of habit, I continued to grab for the barbwire fence at my feet as soon as someone approached too close. It took baby steps to remedy the fear in my head. I repeated positive affirmations to myself over and over—*I am worthy, I am likeable, I am capable of lasting friendships*—until I believed them.

As I continued to rewrite the story I told myself, I left the awkward mom I used to be behind the window curtain.

I started replying *yes* to the invites I had so often declined. My calendar became completely booked up with social events and playdates. My social life became full and fulfilling, leaving me little time to worry about my old self anymore. I mean, I had popsicles to hand out and sunscreen to apply at pool parties in our backyard—I no longer had time to mope around.

As the kids grew older and their social events and extracurricular activities pulled me out into the world, I actually had to start declining invites because my calendar became too full. I was still an introvert at heart and had to take breathers in between all the fun. Eventually, I found the balance I needed—*one night out equals two nights in to fully recover.*

I even initiated a women's splurge group to ensure I had a social outing with girlfriends at least once a month. It was an opportunity for likeminded women to set aside time to have wine and appetizers without kids around. Each member would throw in a small amount of money. We'd draw names, and the winner would spend her earnings on a "splurge" item of her choice and host the next month's party. I thoroughly enjoyed having girlfriends to laugh with—those visits were good for the soul. I couldn't believe I had gone so long without those types of friendships.

I spent so many of my younger years trying to acclimate into certain groups—mostly to the popular girl groups. But the kicker was, no matter how hard I tried, I'd probably never be the cheerleader type—it just wasn't in my genes. I liked wearing funky-coloured glasses, catching up on the latest non-fiction reading list, and making to-do lists that could drive a Type Z personality up the wall. I was the intelligent, witty introvert, who actually enjoyed watching *The Golden Girls* reruns.

When I finally felt what true belonging was, I felt okay to sit in my own skin. It was the most incredible feeling to belong, *finally*. I became a groupie in my own club and the rest just fell into place. I quit trying to win the approval of outsiders and I focused on belonging to those who loved me *all* of the time. I was a mean, lean, healing machine, being restored in ways I never could have imagined.

When I found acceptance in the women's splurge group, I was finally able to fully let go of my electric fence. I let go of the need to fit in and be accepted by colleagues, peers, and even old friends. If they were real friends, they'd stay. If they weren't, well, that was good for my soul, too.

When I opened the doors to my dusty inner closet, my new circle of friends accepted every fault, moth, and skeleton hidden in the darkest of corners. And they didn't just accept me—I was given a standing ovation for my bravery and spirit in becoming my true self. The friends that stayed, and the friends that came, offered unconditional support with no sort of judgement attached. No one ever tried to fix any of my issues—they listened and held space for me with an open heart. I never felt inadequate or condemned for speaking my truth.

And better yet, my light became a bright beacon for other weirdos to flock to. But we didn't seem like weirdos, because we all fit so well together. That weirdo beacon made the process of searching for friends automatic. People with the same vibration—wanting to have fun, evolve, and learn—came knocking on my door, asking for my friendship. *Step right in, friend.*

Once I had a friend circle to lean on, I was finally comfortable enough to address the relationship with myself. To fully heal, I'd have to accept myself for everything I was, *and* everything I wasn't. It would be the most important relationship I'd uncover during my entire five-year healing journey.

I didn't have an overarching catalyst to bring about this change, so I went searching for assistance. The course that appealed most to me was titled *Rebuild Your Life*, a weekend workshop addressing the roots of trauma and then living out your best life. It sounded like exactly what I needed. *Where can I sign up?*

The workshop was scheduled for a weekend in May, which in the agriculture industry, is terrible timing for both our business and my work schedule—I'd be overworked and single parenting. It was also being held in a city about three hours away. I could have found any number of excuses not to attend, but I did no such thing. I was in the midst of creating my own love story and nothing could get in my way.

I typed in my credit card digits and pressed enter. *There you have it, universe. I've paid for the course, now find a way to get me there.* Making my happiness and self-worth a priority was no longer optional—it was a final puzzle piece to finish the entire puzzle of the life I was trying to piece together. And guess what?

It worked.

My challenge to the universe paid off. At the last minute, doors magically opened. The course location was switched to be held in the city near where I lived, allowing me to get to the course with ease. Mike suddenly had the weekend off and could watch the kids. *I hear you, universe. Thanks for confirming this for me.*

I was seated at a table with four other attendees. As I waited for the workshop to begin, I made stilted conversation, nervously wondering how much interactive audience participation would be required. Could I possibly do the deep inner work I needed to do in the company of strangers? What would they think if I was asked to reveal some of my wicked inner secrets?

The course instructor began the day by asking us to bravely step out of our comfort zones. She demystified the Law of Attraction, teaching the group how to focus on our desires rather than our limiting beliefs, because what we focus on is attracted to us. As these were not new concepts to me, it was more of a refresher. But it was the next section she covered that brought me to my knees.

Before breaking for lunch, she had us pull out the two items she had asked us to bring along—a journal and a picture of ourselves from when we were approximately four years old. We started a meditation, looking at the picture of our younger selves, asking *what would you have me know today?* In the background, she played the song "This is Me" from the inspirational musical *The Greatest Showman.* The anthem of self-acceptance about being brave and bruised and making no apologies for being who I was permeated every cell of my being. My soul was vibrating with new possibilities.

I came into that course wanting what everyone else in the entire world wants—to be accepted. I didn't want to be melted like a witch for being open with my secrets. That open, vulnerable four-year-old girl in the photo was the person I was always meant to be—carefree, lighthearted, and living in truth. I was always there, I had merely lost sight of myself when cultural conditioning got a hold of me.

It was in that moment I discovered the missing puzzle piece to living my best life. The meditation answered the question I had been asking—*can I be this vulnerable to the outside world?* The answer? A deafening yes.

It was okay to be brave and bruised at the same time. It was okay to be vulnerable. It was time to show my true self to the world, without apology. *Watch out world, I'm in the process of blossoming open.*

The room was dark, but I knew the inconsolable tears pouring out of me couldn't be hidden from the others at my table, and found it no longer mattered. *Is it break time yet? Oh, well, hopefully I don't see any of these people again. Flow, baby, flow.*

In one afternoon, I began to uncover my true, authentic self by accepting each one of the flaws and regrets I had tried so desperately to hide during my early adult life. I came into the session frightened to be vulnerable and transparent, but left knowing I could continue to let people into my life.

In addition, I walked out of that course feeling forgiveness towards my old friend from so many years ago. The relationship was over, and I would probably never reciprocate her gestures, but at the very least, I could let bygones be bygones. I had no reason for *not* wanting to reignite the relationship, but I was ready to move forward without it—the experience had taught me what I needed to learn from it. For both my sake and hers, I could leave my anger behind and allow something better to fill the void.

I'm still a project in progress—I'm young and I'm still learning the game. I wish I could tell you life gets better, or easier, or more perfect with practice, but I'd be lying. The truth is, you get smarter. You become better able to handle situations you once could not. It takes a few burnt bridges to learn that it's easier to maintain a relationship than torch and rebuild it, now doesn't it?

My tiny step forward in the forgiveness sector was a start, and it gave me strength to know I could overcome other character problems later on the winding Yellow Brick Road. Life could become an amazing journey if I simply allowed it to be.

As I left that session, I experienced a sense of freedom I had never felt before. It felt as if I had just been to a city built of Emeralds, and I finally knew the secret to finding my way home—it was returning to the person I always was.

Once I came home from the seminar, I made it a priority to address the rest of the debilitating stories in my head. I had already seen how changing the one that was the hardest—my worthiness as a friend—could produce incredible results. From that point on, I began to closely examine all of the details in my life, relationships and material items alike.

Not long after, I came to a full stop in the middle of my living room and stared at my bookshelf.

The bookshelf was the first thing any visitor noticed when they walked through our front door. It was full of books chosen to make me look well read, worldly, and studious. As I stared at the carefully placed contents, I realized my bookshelf represented the story I wanted others to believe about me—a story I had been telling myself since I was a little girl.

I was never the prettiest or the skinniest, but I *was* smart and dependable. So, I ran with the story and created a resume to match. I went to business school, wore dignified glasses, and carried a black briefcase, confident I could play the smart card and win. I relied on my brain to carry me over the threshold of success. My bookshelf was meant to advertise that story to others. My at-home library reflected where I had been and what I had learned over my years of sacrificing happiness. I clung to my books to give me a sense of accomplishment—but that story no longer reflected what I knew would make me happy.

As soon as I realized this, I moved the contents of the bookshelf downstairs where only our family could see them and moved the bookshelf to the other side of the room. I didn't stop loving books—that will be a lifelong love affair—but I no longer had anything to prove to anyone. I had a firm understanding of who I was and what I stood for, and I didn't need a bookshelf to tell me so.

As for the bookshelf? When I went to refill the empty shelves, I wondered what could possibly fill the void. I settled on two pieces of pottery and a fake plant, and then placed two of my favorite pictures in the center—one of our immediate family of four and one of just my boys. Now, when I walk past that shelf, I stop and stare at those photos, amazed at how I could have missed commemorating the most important parts of my life for so long.

Not long after I told my mom this story, she came for a visit. She stood and admired the new arrangement in silence for a few moments, and then declared she liked it better this way. She agreed with me—it was filled with what was important now.

She didn't mean the bookshelf.

She was pointing out the growth she had seen in me over the last few years. She knew I was smart, worthy, and enough, even before I did—and long before I moved the bookshelf.

After the bookshelf revelation, every piece of furniture and item in my house was analyzed for how it reflected the internal renovation I'd been going through. I had come to realize that the external clutter in my home was my internal clutter on display. And if changing on the inside often results in changes in your environment, the reverse is also true—sometimes changing your environment can change your insides, too.

Each holiday season, I hang a new seasonal wreath on my front door. After the *Rebuild Your Life* seminar, I instinctively began hanging them on the inside of my door instead of the outside. I no longer had to impress anyone but myself—internally or externally. (Apparently, neither did my front door.)

Want to see behind my curtains now?

Come on in. My door is wide open, and I promise, there's no bookshelf obstructing your view.

CHAPTER EIGHT

The Magic is in the Click

Taking off my green spectacles and accepting motherhood for everything it was had brought me to a beautiful point in my life. But I still felt as though a piece of the puzzle was missing—I just couldn't quite place it.

Not only was I thriving, but our family life was, too. I had processed the aftereffects of my miscarriages, I had begun the healing process from my eating disorder, and I had begun a new narrative by letting go of old childhood stories I wished to detach from.

So with all of my self-work accomplishments, I was surprised to still feel irritated much of the time. My coffee cup wasn't spilling over anymore, but the edges were stained with residual resentment. I was holding grudges towards those who had brought me to my breaking point in the first place and the fact that their issues—the contents of their own cups—had spilled into my life and caused me so much pain. *Why couldn't they clean up their mess themselves? Why am I the one left standing here with the mop and pail?*

I didn't want to pour the contents of my cup out until I had something to replace it with—and I *knew* what my cup needed most—forgiveness. *Don't we all leave the hardest task for last?* Pouring in forgiveness could replace the remaining liquid of resentment in my cup for good.

We were initially offered our trucking business only months after my two miscarriages. Since Mike had a trucking licence, the opportunity seemed like a perfect fit. This company did only short hauls year-round, which meant he would be home with us every night. With Mike as the dispatcher, he would have the ability to create his own driving schedule, and we'd finally have some predictability with his hours of operation. Owning and operating the business would give us the chance to have a semi-normal family life.

With the recent miscarriages, I was struggling with the idea of returning to my job after Baby Number Two. We had just found out Weston was on the way and I would be looking at another maternity leave in the next year (if all went as I hoped with the pregnancy—which it did, thank God). The offer of the business seemed like a dream come true, opening up the possibility of staying at home with my kids in the future. I knew I could manage the books and invoicing in the convenience of our home. And if I decided to stay at my day job and needed to be away for business travel, Mike could easily schedule himself to be at home.

We had never run a business, there was a hefty price tag, and there was no guarantee of success, but it excited us to our bones. There were so many unknowns, but we were both hard workers and the promise for a better family life beckoned like a ray of hope. So we did what our hearts were telling us to do—we jumped in feet first.

We disagreed on terms with the seller during the acquisition period, mostly about what the company was actually worth. Even after a professional evaluation, the appraised value didn't seem to factor into the seller's final asking price, which we felt was high. Despite the disagreement, we followed through on the acquisition because of the value we saw in it for us—time for our family. Ready to get started on our new enterprise, we wrote the cheque anyway— but I'd be lying if I didn't tell you a smidgen of disappointment simmered beneath my smile.

One of my last in-person meetings with the previous owner happened when we took a picture for an announcement of new ownership of the company for the local newspaper. We met at a local Dairy Queen diner, chosen because the restaurant parking space was large enough to park a few large semis. I smiled for the camera alongside the seller and the other drivers in the company, and then Bentley and I patiently waited in the car, waiting for Mike. When the photo shoot was completed, the seller invited Bentley and me to go into the restaurant for a cherry sundae with him and his wife.

Still guarded from our previous discussions, I declined, saying we'd wait for Mike in the parking lot and then go home. But instead of heading into the restaurant, he stayed and chatted with us while Mike finished speaking to the other drivers. Despite my resentment, the conversation grew lighter, and I even laughed a few times. When Mike approached us, ready to go, the man said, "See, we could have had an ice cream without the mosquito bites by now."

It was the last conversation I ever had with him.

Shortly after, he called to inform us he had cancer. Mike took the call. I could see the worry in Mike's eyes and I could hear the man's words through the receiver.

Time stopped for me. My heart sank as I realized that the last time I'd spoken to him, I'd been pasting on a false smile to hide my disappointment. I'd been busy resenting someone who had only been trying to provide for his family in the only way left available to him.

Within months of that call, he passed away. Instead of attending a retirement party, we attended his funeral. It was held on my last day of work before my maternity leave with Weston was set to begin. Between the transition to this next phase of life, the pregnancy hormones, and this new loss, I was emotional, to say the least.

As I sat there listening to the funeral eulogy, I couldn't help but feel regret for the reactions I'd had towards the entire situation.

Why didn't I accept the cherry sundae? It was his peace offering, and I had been too bull-headed to take it. And now I couldn't.

Had I known he'd be gone within months, I would have done things better. I would have taken him less seriously and let go of some of my resentment. I thought I had *time* to do all of those things. After all, no one had forced us to buy the business. It had been our choice, so that feeling of resentment? *That* was all on me.

After the funeral, we went to visit relatives that lived close to where the funeral took place, and picked up our second vehicle, which had been sitting in their yard. Waddling on heels all afternoon while eight months pregnant had exhausted me and I felt I couldn't manage to drive home too, so I accepted my relative's offer to take me home.

During the drive, I held back tears and asked him if he held any regrets. He quickly mumbled *nope* and that was it—one word and done. I took a deep breath, stunned, and thought of what a dangerous, and immediate, statement that was. There was just no thought that went into it—to live a life without regrets? To not have any mistakes to learn or evolve from? I mean, we all have things we've done and later regretted—haven't we? How could he say he had none?

I stewed over his answer for a long time, trying to understand the complexity behind it. Then it occurred to me that it wasn't so much he hadn't made mistakes—it might just be that he wouldn't go back and change them. He had learned to be content with the life he lived by letting go of guilt and shame. He had learned how to move on.

And that's when I knew—I didn't want to live with the poison of anger and resentment anymore. I wanted to live a life without regrets. But to do that, I would need to let go of the resentment I harboured towards those who had hurt me the most.

I wanted to learn how to move on.

The unexpected death of the previous business owner taught me that retirement is not a promised end—none of us know how much time we have left. Life is this precious and unpredictable thing we often take for granted. If I wanted to leave this earth without regrets, I'd have to hurry to take the steps to forgive before my clock ran out, whether I was ready to do so or not.

I *wanted* to move forward, I *wanted* to forgive—but it would take me several years from that eye-opening moment in the car to even begin addressing some of the limiting beliefs that held me back.

My healing session with the medicine woman two years after the funeral would be my second turning point, opening my mind with some baby steps of how to move forward. The *Rebuild Your Life* course, occurring a year after *that* session, would finally help to solidify my process of accepting wholeness beyond brokenness.

From both of those healing sessions, I took away one thought in particular—forgiveness for everyone, not just myself, was the key to replacing anger in life. Finding and learning to live with forgiveness was the last bit of the recipe in my pursuit to wholeness. If I could learn how to forgive and truly let go, I could spend my time filling my cup with more useful items—love and kindness.

After the healing session with the medicine woman, I jotted down the names of people who, in my mind, had created my original brokenness in the first place. My close relative with their pointing finger and thoughtless words. The fourteen-year-old boy in my class who had mumbled thunder thighs under his breath and in my direction. My high school friend who had rejected me. The memories all hurting, affecting, and condemning.

I prioritized the names that affected me most—the people towards which I harboured the deepest lingering resentment. *Hmm* . . . Who should I deal with first? When I had finally narrowed the names down to two, I was shocked to see who had made the top of the list.

God.

Me.

I stared at the list in bewilderment, uncertain how to proceed.

How could I forgive God when I couldn't talk to him in person? And how could I go about forgiving myself?

My naive self had blamed God for causing my initial brokenness. I was taught nothing bad would ever happen to me if I was a good person with strong faith, and it felt as if he hadn't held up his end of that bargain. The way I saw it, had I never gone through my miscarriages, I never would have broken. You'd be watching Netflix right now instead of reading this book, because Chapter One wouldn't exist.

And *me?*

I blamed myself for the mess I was in. I was disappointed in myself for what I had allowed to happen to me and how I had—or hadn't—reacted. I'd never had the confidence to stand up for myself. I was a meek little mouse, saying nothing in my own defense when someone would say something hurtful to me. Instead of dealing with my pain, I had developed an eating disorder to compartmentalize my emotions.

But when forgiveness came a-knocking, I couldn't have orchestrated a more beautiful result. The processes of forgiving both God and myself were both purely accidental and brilliant—almost as magical as discovering the witch of resentment could be melted away with a mere bucket of water.

Forgiveness towards God is wrapped up in the tissue paper of each baby gift bundle I give to every expectant mother I love. The gift always contains at least one of the same three luxury baby items—a WubbaNub baby soother, an Aden + Anais receiving blanket, or a Jellycat stuffed bunny. As valuable as these items are, the lessons I learned from them are priceless to me.

We never seemed to have a shortage of any type of necessity growing up, but I remember that whenever the subject of money came up, it was clear there was no room in the budget for frivolities. My parents often expounded on the fact that money was a precious commodity. It was to be acquired through honest, hard work, and once you had it, it was to be put up on a pedestal. From those initial thoughts, I had modelled a fear about acquiring and keeping money, and my limiting beliefs around the subject sank in to a core level of my psyche.

As I mentioned earlier, I also feared that since I hadn't done much babysitting growing up and didn't even enjoy playing with children, I might not be a good mother. As a result, when we found out we were expecting for the first time, I was terrified at the prospect of being responsible for another human life besides my own.

The birth of Bentley pushed me into facing both fears simultaneously.

With a new baby in my arms, I suddenly *had* to face my fear of parenting in order to get through our day-to-day life. But I soon found my fears had been baseless—I could do this mom gig, no problem. And if I didn't know how to do something for him, I willingly learned. I would have given anything, even my last breath, for him to have a better life. *That's what good moms do.*

The parent I was readily becoming each day demonstrated I *could* be an exceptional mother—I was doing it without even trying. And if I could do that, perhaps I could let go of my fear of scarcity, too.

Once Bentley settled in with us parent trainees, we began spending a *ton* of money on baby supplies that we weren't prepared for. After the Walmart or Costco cashier rang up the formula, diapers, and baby clothing that were now regular shopping list requirements, the final bills would make me gasp. I'd walk away, my stomach tight and my heart beating fast. *Three hundred and fifty dollars for a few groceries and diapers? How does anyone ever afford nice things after having babies?*

The thought stopped me in my tracks. Where was this fear coming from? We never had any issues paying for what we needed, even now that we'd added a baby to the mix. We could still afford the basics and some extras, too. But this fear of spending money had been my constant companion with every purchase I'd ever made. *Am I actually feeling someone else's fear? And if this fear is not mine, can I release it?*

The simple act of questioning the source of my fear proved to be enough to start letting it go.

Prior to having Bentley, I used to go past lovely displays of beautiful items and admire from a distance, barely even touching them,

144

before looking sadly at the price tag and telling myself I couldn't afford such a splurge. But once I overcame my fear of becoming a good mom and not having enough money, I threw away the idea that I couldn't acquire such luxuries, because, in all reality, I could. I was working and making a decent wage. I could splurge on non-essential items if I desired.

I decided to exercise my new-found freedom from my old thought patterns during a shopping trip to Indigo, the Canadian equivalent of Barnes and Noble and one of my favourite places to window shop. I picked up the softest and most extravagant stuffed animal I could find, a Jellycat stuffed bunny, and then added the elephant WubbaNub soother sitting next to it to my stash. I wanted to add the Aden + Anais blanket set, but restrained myself. *One thing at a time, Susie Q.*

I purchased the lavish baby gifts I used to think I couldn't afford. As I walked away from the cash register, I left behind my bondage to a scarcity mindset. I left the store telling myself two things—*I am not my limiting beliefs, I can attract financial abundance if I think differently about money. And two, I'm not only a good mom, I'm an exceptional mom.*

I continued to work on my limiting beliefs around money by purchasing items I had always wanted, but had abstained from buying—Matt & Nat purses, Lululemon clothing, tickets to live concerts, excursions to Disney. Within our budget, if I really wanted something or desired to go somewhere, I purchased or booked it on a whim. *Bye, bye, limiting belief. Hello, Mickey Mouse!*

But when it came to buying the same two baby items during my pregnancy with Weston, I couldn't do it—not because I didn't think we could afford it, though.

I didn't believe the pregnancy would actually hold—my trust with God was shattered. God had taken two babies, what would stop him from taking a third? I despised the leverage he held over my life. I kept my faith in the survival of my child on the back-burner and refused to hold a baby shower. I ate my sadness away with doughnuts—I wouldn't allow myself to be happy until my baby was out and safe in my arms.[18]

During my last month of my pregnancy with Weston, I read the book *Wild* by Cheryl Strayed. The book is her memoir about hiking the Pacific Crest Trail, inexperienced and alone, as she grieved her mother's death. One of her passages resonated deeply with me, "Fear begets fear. Power begets power. I willed myself to beget power. And it wasn't long before I actually *wasn't* afraid".†††

It was *the* aha moment in my forgiveness journey.

In my fear over losing my baby, I hadn't allowed myself to spend money on this child in case I miscarried again, or worse yet, in case the baby wasn't born alive. I had spent my entire pregnancy beset by fear of what might happen instead of enjoying the experience of the growing life inside me. My negative thoughts were holding me back from enjoying the present moment.

I was breaking my heart waiting for the worst possible outcome, and I was losing precious moments of joy in the meantime. I considered my choices. I could continue to be miserable and bitter about what had happened, or I could choose love over fear. Fear might beget fear, but so also love begets love, kindness begets kindness, and forgiveness begets forgiveness.

God had already demonstrated his power—I had no control over the outcome of this pregnancy. I could continue to take all of the pre-natal vitamins in the world and do all of the things you're supposed

---

18 Which I know still isn't a guarantee that my baby would be forever mine. But it was the milestone I couldn't see past.

to do to make a healthy baby, but that was it. Whether I liked God's plan or not, life would go on, so I might as well join in on the ride.

I hopped in my car and did the most unnerving thing I could think of—I drove to Indigo to abolish the last of my limiting beliefs by purchasing the Aden + Anais blanket set. *Okay, Susie Q, it's time . . .* I picked up a pink set, hoping for a girl, but ended up leaving the store with a grey one, since the sex of our new baby was still unknown. The purchase of the blanket was an act of faith that my baby would be born whole and healthy.

As I let go of the store door handle, the air filling my lungs smelled fresher and my heart felt lighter. I held back my emotions until I was out of the store, then let my tears of happiness fall to the pavement. My steps fell in time to the mantra *love begets love, kindness begets kindness, and forgiveness begets forgiveness.*

Those very steps out of the store were the first steps I took towards forgiving God and what had happened between us. With each step, I began to invite God back into my life—and started the process of renewing my faith in Him. I knew no matter the outcome, everything would be okay in the end. And if it wasn't, it just wasn't the end yet.

Had I not been challenged, I would have never awoken. My sawdust heart would have never grown into its beautiful new form had I not been required to evolve. While I had been refusing to deal with my pain, God invited me to let him heal *all* of the brokenness inside of me. He kept presenting me with the same two choices—evolve or repeat.

Like any resilient soul would do, I chose the first—I chose to persevere.

I was ignorant to believe I *should* have control of the future. The biggest wake-up call after my loss was realizing how little control

I actually had. God was *never* in the wrong. In my opinion, he was a God of choices and natural consequences, and if he wanted to control everything on a minute level, he never would have given us free will. And if we never experienced hardship, we'd never gain the resilience to withstand any type of difficulty. *Of course his plan had a purpose.*

More than forgiving God, or what happened, I had to accept that there were a lot of unknowns in the future. I couldn't see the whole picture—I could only see a snapshot of my journey, one moment on the Yellow Brick Road, while he was holding the full movie reel of my life. He'd been next to me when I had lost the babies—he had never left my side, but I'd been too angry to see him. Even when I didn't believe in him, there he was, waiting for me to return. And he was right beside me still, walking me to my car that day in the Indigo parking lot.

If I could learn to breathe on God's time, I could start to relax a little. I had already wasted enough time living in fear and trying to control the outcome. From that drive home to the moment Weston was born, I soaked up every last bit of my pregnancy. Each time I saw my new baby gift purchases, I was reminded to let go of a little more of my anger and resentment, but it was still a process. While this episode began my journey of forgiveness towards God, it would not be fully resolved until several years later when I began actively addressing my wounds during my year of writing.

Near the end of my writing period, I met a very good friend for one last coffee and shopping date before she went on her own maternity leave. At the baby boutique, I picked up an Aden + Anais blanket set and smiled, thinking of my renewed relationship with God. As I handed the gift to my friend, I realized that I was doing it with light, untainted joy. I no longer felt resentment towards God for my miscarriages—I was thankful he was in my life. Nor did I carry limiting beliefs towards money or my ability to parent well. It took time, nearly three years, but I had healed and evolved into a better soul, and my new heart knew it.

So, when you receive a baby gift from me and pull out one of the three items I give to all of my pregnant friends, know that I'm not gifting the material items in the bag. I'm giving the deeper riches I hope to offer to any new mother and her baby—love, perseverance, and the power to forgive.

The accidental forgiveness process towards God taught me that life's circumstances are not always going to be ideal. You're going to lose people you love, sometimes quicker than you're ready for. You're going to have things happen to you that you won't necessarily want to deal with. But when they do happen, I want you to be ready for them. And here's what you need to know: The only thing you have complete control over when these types of situations arise is your reaction. You will not be able to control all of your circumstances, but the ways you choose to move forward from them will always be in your power. You are responsible for your own journey of healing.

You get to decide how bitter or happy you continue to be until your clock times out. No one except you can hold that much authority. You get to decide which version of the story you end up telling yourself and the reality you end up living. And trust me, from my own experience, living with love is a much happier choice.

Allow yourself to be sad or infuriated, but then allow yourself to heal. Give yourself the time and grace to heal from the wounds that suffocate you—don't think you have to rush your process. It took me years to heal, and even when I knew I *wanted* to, it took me another few years to enter a course that would give me the tools to actually follow through on the idea. You are the only person who suffers when you let pain and sadness permeate your life. For your own sake and happiness, choose to hit the *evolve* button, and not the *repeat* one.

Know you don't have to bear your sorrow alone. Instead of hoarding it in your heart, learn to let your sadness go by allowing the outside world to bear some of its weight. The writing of this book and the release of these words into the world has done just that for me. By sharing the weight of my past with the world, I have received the most beautiful gift in return—the opportunity to move forward as a lighter soul.

Forgiving God was only one step of my healing journey. There was still one more person I had to forgive, the hardest one of all . . . myself.

By the time of the shopping trip for baby gifts with my friend, I was in a space of willingness to heal all other existing wounds. *Well, if the wound is open, I might as flush it with hydrogen peroxide, right?*

I knew my name was still on the "to-forgive" list, but the task seemed daunting and much more difficult. It wasn't merely surface work, like greasing a rusty old Tin Woodman—the job would require heart[19] work. I didn't know it then, but the process of forgiving myself would also help restore one of the most important relationships in my life—the relationship with my sister, Jennifer.

Growing up, I had been quite close with Jennifer, who is only three years older than me. But as adults, we had grown apart after

---

19 Yes, *heart* work, not hard work. You know, like the Tin Woodman. I thought I'd clarify for you just because both of my editors questioned it, too.

we had married, built careers, and had children. Life—and its unpredictable turns of events—got in the way of our former relationship. Jennifer's journey to motherhood wasn't easy, and the experience to get there left her with her own grief and anger to deal with. We all get our own Yellow Brick Road, and there is no *right* way to walk it.

I wanted to be there for her, but she had formed an imaginary wall between us, shutting me out of her life like a modern-day Elsa and Anna story. Her continual rejection hit me like a blow to the stomach each time, sending me into the recurring nightmare of when my old friend rejected me at the age of sixteen. When Jennifer rejected me, it seemed as though all of the people I loved dearly—the ones I was most vulnerable to—would always end up pushing me away. I thought it was me, and not them. I made it part of my truth.

So I built a fortified, icy version of my sister's wall so *no one* could ever hurt me again—not a friend, not a sister, not another soul. Once she began her own healing journey, she approached me many times to try to remedy our relationship. But I was deeply hurt and wedged under the limiting belief I held so dearly—I am not worthy of having good friends.

For years after, our relationship never went beyond exchanging pleasantries. Even despite the resolutions I'd made after the man who had sold us our trucking company had died, I found it was easier said than done to let go of old hurts. I *knew* I should forgive her, but I didn't want to.

The catalyst for healing our relationship came when I read the book *Marrow: A Love Story* by Elizabeth Lesser. The book is a mesmerizing love story between two sisters uncovering their journey to forgiveness with each other through the life-and-death experience of a bone marrow transplant. For the best chance of a successful transplant, both sisters wanted to clear the air over past disagreements between each other. They thought the transplant would be more successful if their relationship could be healed first.‡‡‡

I read the book in a complete trance, staying up the entire night. Through chapter after chapter, I resonated with the author's story. Finally, I closed the back cover and set the book beside me, knowing it was time to set aside the wall of trifling differences that had separated me from my own sister over the last decade.

I thought of the man who'd offered me a cherry sundae and who had died before I ever accepted the peace offering. I never wanted a life-or-death situation to make Jennifer and I realize we had waited too long. His untimely death taught me to accept peace offerings when they are first offered—as you never really know when your last chance to accept them might be.

For years, not only had Jennifer offered me a double cherry sundae, she had served it alongside a Peanut Buster Parfait topped with a banana split apology. I was being *way* too stubborn and was wasting precious time over nothing.

But every good renovation must start with some demolition, right? We needed to get to the root of what had come between us before we could begin to rebuild. It began slowly—a call here, a text there, an offer to babysit each others' kids. But total forgiveness didn't occur until I started taking responsibility for what I, too, had done wrong in the relationship. True resolution of our past hurts began when *I* chose to move beyond my mistakes. I put on a dust mask and grabbed the largest sledge hammer I could find to collapse the final, and imaginary, barrier between us. That's when things started to rapidly move forward.

The renovation of our relationship was completed at a gorgeous lakeside tourist town in the heart of Saskatchewan.

For her birthday, Jennifer's husband surprised her with a weekend away in a rented cabin at a camping resort town that is so removed from civilization, you can't even get consistent cell phone coverage. She invited my mother, my older sister, Pamela, and me to join her. For the first time in a long time, we had the opportunity to spend time together to decompress and connect.

When I received the invitation, there was no internal debate on whether or not to go. My journey to wholeness was about embracing all of the *what ifs*, and this situation was no different. Without any misgivings, I left all of my responsibilities with my husband and headed to the lake.

I drove up with Pamela. As we parked in the rustic cabin's driveway, we could see through the window that mom and Jennifer had already arrived and were busily unpacking groceries in the kitchen. My stomach twisted, and I wondered how many more chances I'd have to clear the air with Jennifer. *What if this is the last weekend getaway where everyone in this group is alive? How would I want to spend my last precious days with them?* I hoped for an opportunity to make things right at last.

We settled in and unpacked for the weekend.

The next morning, to celebrate our first day at the lake together, we went shopping along the lakefront strip of businesses that cater exclusively to the summer crowd of tourists. It was there, in the tiniest of boutiques, that we stumbled upon the Magic Romper.

Jennifer initially grabbed the outfit, coming out of the fitting room to model it for us—served with a pivot and a hip shake. Her entire act was so adorable, I snatched an identical one to see if it would look just as good on me.

When I waltzed out of the fitting room dressed in the matching, flowered romper, we both burst out laughing. Being particularly fond of the movie *The Sisterhood of the Traveling Pants*, I immediately thought we had found our version of the jeans shared by the four friends in the story, but in romper form. I suggested we buy the same outfit for the upcoming family wedding we were to attend at the end of summer.

That evening, Jennifer pulled out all of the essentials for a Girls Night In—wine, face masks, nail polish, and even a detox footbath. Pamela, Mom, and I were all content with just visiting without the need for a spa, but Jennifer's immediate disappointment with our reactions was all over her face. And it was *her* birthday, after all.

That was *the* moment.

I internally called a truce and reached out for the double-stacked cherry sundae.

I jumped in—almost literally—by sinking my feet into a bubbling footbath and slathering my face in a green mask.

My mother looked at me in surprise. "What are you doing?"

Pouring myself a glass of wine, I replied, "Well, I'm participating, of course."

An immediate smile came to Jennifer's face.

I loved my sister with all my heart—she wasn't just my fairy godmother, she was my Glinda. When things got tough, guess whose number was on speed dial? She was there for every tear-filled confession of motherhood, marriage, and everything in-between over the last ten years of our rocky relationship. It was wrong of me to shut her out when she needed me, too.

Being the older sister and the first to experience many of the heartaches I'd also encountered, she had already taken the lead on knowing how and when to move on. So now that I was finally reciprocating her initiative, she didn't hesitate. She grabbed a glass of wine from the kitchen counter and began applying nail polish next to me. Without a word being said between either of us, a truce had been called, and we both knew it. Jen had been waiting for me, and I was now ready.

Beginning to reconcile with Jennifer filled me with so much contentment and peace that it made me want to forgive myself, too. *What if I could feel this good all of the time, even towards myself? What if addressing my relationship with myself could make every other relationship fall into place, like this one has?*

What if forgiving myself enables me to forgive everyone else on my list?

The medicine woman had told me that healing was one hundred percent my own responsibility, no matter what or who caused the baggage, and she had been right—healing was all on me. I couldn't change the past, but I could change my future by releasing what tied me to the people who hurt me the most.

I let go of the illusion that my life could have been any different had I been stronger or more confident, and I accepted that I wasn't necessarily going to get the apology I hoped for in every situation. The people who hurt you the most generally have no idea of the life-altering cracks they leave within you.

The fourteen-year-old boy who said I had thunder thighs or the relative who said I was thick-boned had no idea their words could send me into a swirling decline for over a decade. Honestly, they might very well be unaware they even said anything wrong— hurtful words often come from ignorance and insensitivity more than deliberate malice. I mean, how many times have we all said something foolish, and then moved on, without an apology to the person you said it to? For me, it's a *lot*.

The forgiveness I had to give had nothing to do with them, but it had everything to do with me. And defining what the fibrous roots of forgiveness looked like to me allowed me to start to make peace with my past. I forgave myself for not having the emotional maturity to deal with hurtful comments I received at the age of six, eleven, and fourteen. I began to forgive myself for every regret and mistake that had come thereafter, looking at them as learning curves that had brought me to where I am today.

My flaws were a part of me—without them, my story would be incomplete. Like every other human being on this earth, I was always going to be a person with a past—miscarriages, eating disorder, parenting insecurities, limiting beliefs, and regrets. But if I embraced them as pillars for developing me into who I had become, their shackle of shame couldn't have as tight of a hold.

Forgiveness felt good and letting go of harboured resentment and anger was freeing. I couldn't believe I hadn't done this sooner. If I had, I could have been living like this all along.

Before leaving the cabin the next morning, we checked each room to ensure no items were left behind. I took the keys and offered to close up the cabin—I had one last thing to do. Swinging the door slightly to reach the coat rack behind it, I hung up the flawed, wounded self-image I had carried with me for so long. I no longer required that protective suit of armour to keep me safe from the world or to help me stand up for myself. I had healed my old wounds and I could continue to walk forward with vulnerable strength.

I embodied the characteristics of a wicked enchantress, but also those of a young protagonist in her own restorative journey. I was both beautifully flawed and utterly fabulous.

As we climbed into the car, I smiled, finally understanding how those two qualities could coincide. I did the most natural thing next—I accepted myself for everything I was and everything I wasn't. I adjusted my sunglasses and turned up the tunes for the journey home.

The next time I saw Jennifer, we were dressed in our matching rompers at the family wedding. I will always cherish the photo taken of us together that night, our arms around each other's shoulders. There are just some pictures in your life that you keep close to your heart. (I keep it next to the one with me in a bikini holding Bentley on the beach in Nova Scotia.)

The magic potion of forgiveness was all around us. Our hug held so many words—*I'm sorry for everything that did and didn't happen between us. Let's move forward.* It was a hug of support, a hug of tenderness, and a hug of sisterhood. It was the hug we had both been waiting nearly a decade for.

We rocked the night away in our heels and matching outfits. We danced, we twirled, and we had fun—just like in the old days. The icy barrier we had formed vanished into thin air. But not only were *we* back, *I* was back, too. I wasn't only wearing a magic romper anymore, I was wearing a vulnerable suit of forgiveness—and those things are a *lot* lighter than a suit of armour.

I'd left my suit of armour hanging on a hook in a rustic cabin, hundreds of miles away. Without that weight, I was free to dance with abandon to every song of the evening. And with each dance, I embraced my ridiculous awesomeness and began shining like the supernova I was.

I awoke the next morning, smiling and relaxed in the morning sunshine that radiated through the glass window panes. As my outstretched arms grazed the headboard, the words *I'm back* came out of my mouth. I was becoming my true self and blossoming into the person I was always supposed to be.

I was creating my very own fairy-tale story, but in real life. Like Dorothy in *The Wonderful Wizard of Oz*, I had discovered that the power to return home had been with me all along—I just had to take the hard way to learn it. If I would have taken the easy route, I never would have absorbed the lessons I needed to learn to come back to myself. But now that I had found the magic, I simply had to use it.

Click, click, click.

CHAPTER NINE

The Long Road Home

I huddled on my bed in the dark, the province-wide power outage and my rising anxieties pressing against my spirit as the house grew colder and colder. I had been blogging about my healing journey for three months, and still, here I was, in the midst of a full-blown anxiety attack. What if the power didn't come back on before breakfast? Were the kids warm enough? Did we even have any instant coffee in the house, just in case? What if the power stayed out all day and the pipes burst? How would I work without electricity?

The lack of illumination and heat in our house echoed the way our lives felt. Everything in my daily life already seemed to be a struggle, and now we had no power on top of it? *Come on, universe! How can I heal from past problems when you keep piling on new ones? Give. Me. A. Break.*

But as I lay there, I thought about how far I'd already come. I was no longer a broken vessel or a resentment-spilling coffee cup. The panic attack in the dark was one of the final defenses of my doomed, old self, and there was no number of universal obstacles[20]

---

20 Including ravenous wolves, wild crows, or buzzing bees for that matter . . .

that could slow me down. I was the youthful heroine of my own story, rising from the destruction path of a cyclone. I was leaving my wounded past with renewed faith, grace, and intent.

For several years, but especially since I had that session with the holistic medicine woman seven months before, I had been addressing the stories that both shaped and shamed me, learning how to simultaneously love and forgive myself and others around me. I was no longer a victim to what had gone before.

That didn't mean I was perfect—far from it. But I was moving forward. I was becoming whole. And, through my regular blog posts, I was sharing with others what I'd learned. Even when I fell down, even when I stumbled, I'd keep writing until I could say, "I'm better. I'm healed. And the world needs to know what I've learned."

As I thought about the steps I'd already taken on my journey, the cold darkness that oppressed me lifted. Sunrise was on the horizon, brightening our home and my spirit in a single moment. *I can do this, I can heal.* But first, I'd have to start the day.

Mike and I dressed the kids and got ready to take them to daycare and then headed into the garage to leave. With the jubilation of my renewed resolve, I had completely forgotten we still didn't have power. The garage door would have to be opened manually.

Now, on a normal day, I'd classify manually opening the door as a *blue* job. I'd have played dumb and acted as if it was something I couldn't possibly do. *Mike, come save me! Grab your axe and rescue me from the witch's tower where I am oh-so-helpless, now won't you? Watch out for the wolves surrounding the fortress.* But my newfound fearlessness wouldn't let me ask for help this time. I'd have to start saving myself on all levels if I wanted to heal properly. I stepped towards the garage door.

Mike stood watching me, his head tilted to the side. He raised his eyebrows, baffled at my sudden attempt to do something so out of the norm. He watched my five-foot-two stature jump, fumble, and finally grab the inside string hanging from the middle of the garage ceiling to manually unlock the door, an action he could have done easily himself.

I gave a heave on the handle. And suddenly it happened—I succeeded in saving myself.

With an upward thrust of the cold and heavy door, sunlight came streaming into the dark garage, blinding me. Those beautiful beams of light cascading through the open doorway were a sign of my redemption in progress. I let the sunlight pour into my being, filling up all the cracks that had reappeared during the cold, dark night with molten gold.

I was no longer Humpty Dumpty of broken pottery, an egg laying on the ground in pieces. I was the woman repaired with gold, brilliantly shining for the world to see.

I immediately knew I'd be okay. Mike and I would be okay. Our family would be okay. No matter how any of our present struggles turned out, everything would turn out just fine. And later that night, I blogged about how the next time I found myself sitting in a cold bedroom in the dark, I'd plan to make the best of the situation. I'd plan to teach my children how to not be afraid of the dark. *Come light the candles and let's play UNO.*

Seeing Mike watch me open the door reaffirmed the support around me if I needed someone to lean on in my journey ahead. *I wasn't alone in this.* My internal struggles were my own, but Mike would be here if and when I needed him. We were in this marriage together and all of our puzzle pieces would figure themselves out eventually.

I stepped inside the house to grab one last item before leaving home. At that moment, the lights in our house switched on, and the buzzing of electronics filled the air as though nothing out of the ordinary had just occurred—no power outage, no anxiety attack, nor a triumphant discovery of the need to fully heal. I was suddenly filled with a sense of calm.

However, while all of our modern conveniences resumed their normal cycles, something had also clicked on internally, continuing me on a voyage of self-revitalization. The ghosts of my past could no longer hide from me if I greeted them in the hallway with a lamp in hand. I could survive *any* power outage if I steadied myself enough to sit bravely in the dark. The light always turns back on—it simply takes a little faith that it will.

Beyond all of my self-discoveries that morning, the power outage revealed some of the more practical things I needed to take care of. In my moment of crisis, I had concluded our family was not prepared for an apocalypse, so on the way home, I planned to pick up a few essentials to keep on hand for the next emergency. You know, essentials like canned goods, bottled water, and instant coffee. I mean, give a girl a break—*first I drink the coffee, and then I do the things.*

Especially during an apocalypse.

When I began my Year of Writing, I didn't know that's what it would become. But once I started, I couldn't stop. Divine guidance overtook the process, and I became a mere vessel for the words. There was an incredible amount of simplicity in writing out my story—I didn't have to *try* to write, the words naturally flowed from pen to paper. As I acknowledged my flaws and regrets, inauthentic bits of debris fell away like the remaining dust of a sculpture taking shape. By exposing my brokenness for all to see, those stories no longer held power over me.

My cup of spilled-over coffee was the best thing to ever happen to me—it drained my shameful contents and enabled me to refill it with something incredibly more fulfilling. My cup is now overflowing with joy, gratefulness, and love. Ironically, my journey taught me the most useful state of a cup is when it is empty. Once you empty your cup, you have full control of what to fill it with.

I became a mother while on a mountaintop of accomplishments and achievements, and it woke me up to reality. Experiencing loss as a mother pushed me off the mountainous, rocky top edge, into my own witch's lair. As painful as it was, that's where all the most valuable lessons of my life unearthed themselves—as I lay at the bottom of the mountainside in a dark hole with no ladder in sight.

I ended up building that ladder, one rung at a time, as I uncovered my true self. Each step on the ladder was a lesson learned through raising my children and seeing my flawed self through their eyes. Over time, I found enchanted clues in the middle of the laundry heap and healing moments while racing around to get my children to school and daycare, and me to work on time.

Motherhood broke me, but it's also what *saved* me. If I'd never had my children, I likely never would have toppled off that mountain, blissfully unaware of the trials that would have been mine—but I never would have climbed back to the top, whole and healed and stronger than ever before. I never would have melted the witch that had hounded me along the Yellow Brick Road. I am now a different person, a *better* person—empathetic, kind, brave, content, and whole.

Rejecting the world's projected version of myself was strenuous, hard labour—healing was *not* an easy task. And once I climbed back up the mountain, the delicate air reaffirmed that life, in all aspects, wasn't going to simply show up for me—I'd have to continue to show up for it. Even though I had traded in my boring, black heels for sparkly red ones, I still had to use will, intent, and action to get what I needed out of life. I'd have to continue climbing if I wanted to complete the looming bucket list items on my overflowing vision board.

Feeling wholeness within created presence in my everyday life. I embraced *every* morning I woke up with my babies in my bed, Lego indents and all. I held their hugs longer, rushed them out of the car and into their schools less. I was okay with being late for work in exchange for an extra snuggle. The limited time I had left with them was squeezed into every possible moment. I didn't want to miss another second of the little things in life.

But I wanted to do more than simply live my life—I wanted to live it on purpose. It was time to start stepping in the direction I wanted to be in a month, a year, and five years down the road.

I've been to more funerals than I'd like to count, and they often included an intimate slideshow of the life of the deceased. I remember sitting through one of these thinking *what if that's all we really have when we check out—a frantic ten-minute slideshow to remember us by? What will my funeral slideshow look like? Will I look fulfilled and happy in my slides?*

I internalized that none of us get out of here alive—not a single one of us. As I sat there watching the slideshow, I promised myself that when my expiry date was up, I'd leave this world with a bang. Now, I have to admit that my life up until then hadn't been that spectacular. I wanted to change that. I wanted to have an exceptional exit slideshow to remember me by. But what should be on it?

Instead of recreating the wheel, like the true millennial I am, I enlisted Google to help me find the answers. What did strangers regret most at the end of their lives? I'd add their wish-I'd-done items to my bucket list and turn them into I-will-dos instead.

The simplicity of the lists I pulled up stunned me. People regretted not having enough courage to passionately take life by the horns. They wished they had worried less and had taken more risks. They regretted they hadn't travelled more or lived more extravagantly while saving less for their retirement. They wished they would have been less absent in their children's lives, working less during their children's younger years. They wished they would have been more honest and would have forgiven more. They wished they would have stopped chasing the wrong things. They wished they would have lived more presently.

I was thrilled to see the easiness of these tasks—I could do all of this, and more. *Be yourself, pursue your passion, listen to your heart's desires, care less about what other people think, stay in your own lane, say what you really want to say and do what you really want to do. Got it.*

Even if life's events decided to push me off my mountain again, I'd have the tools to help me slide down it instead of free-falling this time. Filling my slideshow could be a pleasurable adventure.

As a young twenty-something entering the corporate world, I had thought I knew what I wanted—to climb the corporate ladder, become successful, and to receive the approbation of others. Like the Scarecrow, Cowardly Lion, and Tin Woodman, I was looking for someone else to give me the fulfillment I yearned for, not realizing that doing so was not within their power. When I finally got to where I was going, all I ended up with were some pseudo-courage, a sawdust heart, and a whole lot of brand-new brains—in other words, cheap imitations of what I truly needed.

But after I became a mother, wholeness began to occupy my heart space. My desires transformed into something much more meaningful. And I finally came to understand that what I needed to be happy could never be given to me by magic, or a wizard for that matter. Those distinguishing qualities and traits had to be developed and earned. They were found within when I ventured forth on my quest through the winding road of motherhood.

Along the Yellow Brick Road, I had found the wisdom to know what I needed, the courage to become who I needed to be, and the compassion to love myself and others better. Most importantly, I had learned to follow my heart to find my way home.

I could now trust my heart's decisions to fill up my funeral slideshow. I started making a bucket list of activities that made my heart happy. If my heart said *yes*, the event or action was a go. If my heart said *no*, I moved on to the next adventure. *Next, please.*

Synchronizing my goals and ambitions with my new priorities allowed me to start living a soul-driven life rather than an ego-driven life. My heart decisions didn't always make sense, and sometimes, I'd even find myself fighting them as they actively played out. I'd often ask myself if I was allowed to have that much fun. It was hard to wrap my head around enjoying myself after being so serious for the last part of my life. But my previous experiences of loss made me more sensitive to life's fragility and fleeting nature. I stopped placing my faith in the idea that tomorrow would come and instead started doing *all* of the things today.

I immediately stopped clowning around with the relationship with my children. My time with them was extremely limited—if Weston decided to leave our home at the age of eighteen that meant

I only had fourteen years left with my youngest at home. *That isn't a lot of time.* I made play a priority over work and the cleanliness of the house. I worried less about the paint on the floor and more about the masterpieces we created. *Let there be scratches on the kitchen table and chips in the drywall.*

Work naturally fell into second place after my family. I would still be the mom who would volunteer at my kids' school events with cupcakes in hand—even if they were store-bought. I decided if work didn't like the new life balance, I'd have to leave and find another job. I was an exceptional employee and any company would be lucky to have a firecracker like me.

The concessions I'd have to make to do both roles—Mommy Extraordinaire and Boss Babe—were not going to be Insta-worthy. My post of me playing with my kids might reveal my frizzy hair. *The perfect shot* for my social media feed might expose a messy house in the background.

My feeds showed that I was finally okay with the mess that came with being a busy working mom. Instead of endlessly scrolling through the curated lives of others on Facebook, I decided to just start making the most of my own. And when I did, outsiders were grateful for my effort to display the realness of what it took to do both worlds—it allowed them to be brave enough to start living their own truths, too.

I allowed fun back into my life, scheduling regular girls' nights, date nights with my husband, and family game nights. Laughter became regular medicine in our household. Dance parties happened every day, and not just on special days. I came home from nights out with friends with my cheeks hurting from laughing too hard. And instead of counting calories while I had been out, I'd had a few extra glasses of wine before I left. I used the fancy dinnerware in my house every day. *What was I waiting for, my funeral luncheon?*[21]

When I really wanted something, I saved or sacrificed other things to be able to afford it. Travel was a priority to me, so I accepted the compromises of driving an older vehicle and living in a smaller home to be able to factor it into our lives. I allowed financial abundance into my life when I started saying *yes* to the items I really could afford (i.e. Jellycat stuffed bunnies), but always thought I couldn't due to my limiting belief system around money.

You and I are not guaranteed time or our health—we are as wealthy as our health is. I hate to break it to you, but even if you do everything in your power to live a long life—stringent fitness regime, healthy diet, added supplements, and a protein shake every morning—you may not be able to enjoy your dreams when you *think* it's time to start enjoying them.

I repeat—life is *not* going to wait for you.

It's short and fast, like an exhilarating ride on a rollercoaster. The ride starts with a monumental plunge, a gasp for air, and a beginning beat in your heart, pounding in excitement. As you grow, you may even be frightened or anxious as you follow the uncertain track of life. You might enter dark caves and tunnels and experience turns and twists without warning.

And right when you think you have a handle on its tracking system and start having fun, the ride will abruptly end. Your head will jolt forward, the bar will be raised, and you'll see the exit sign ahead. Even if you're not ready, when your time is up, you must get off.

---

21 While we're on the topic, I'd like egg salad sandwiches served at my funeral luncheon. There, Mike, now it's in writing.

You might think, *I'm young. I've got plenty of time.* And you might. But you might die tomorrow, so start doing what you want to do today. I keep a measuring tape on my vision board that helps me remember that life is precious. It's just a flexible measuring tape for sewing that I bought at the Dollar Store, but it represents how many years I might expect to live if I fulfill the average lifespan of eighty years. I cut it down to only what I can reasonably expect to remain, and each year, I snip another centimetre off it.

The visual reminder of *how much tape you have left* really puts your time here on earth into perspective. It's why I argue for you to start living your life today and not tomorrow. It's why I don't fool around anymore.

I want to exit from a life well lived. I want the conversations around my casket to sound something like "I'm telling ya, she was one exceptional lady. The world was better because she was in it. And she was fun! Remember that time in Greece when she jumped off a cliff into an ocean full of jellyfish?"[22]

You get my point, right?

In the end, I guarantee to you what will matter to you the most will be little things—the impromptu coffee dates with your dad, the summer nights swinging on the porch with your partner, the infectious toddler laughs that made your belly ache.

The connections you make here on earth are so much more important than the material items you will *ever* accumulate. When it's your time to go, it won't matter what kind of car is in your driveway, trust me. What will matter is the support system surrounding your bed, holding your hand.

---

22 Which actually happened, by the way.

As I speculated how I would want to live and die, my grandparents came to mind. To me, they exemplified what living happily looked like.

My grandparents didn't have a lot of money, so they saved everything—and I mean *everything*. They had grown up in the thirties, and those hard decades that they were raised in had created a very frugal mentality—they wasted very little and wanted less.

We'd spend summers at their lake house, and it always smelled like comfort food and coffee. Their furniture didn't match, nor was their food *ever* gourmet, but the two things that were always full were their fridge and their hearts. My grandpa's motto was *feed my people*, and he sat in eyeshot of his front door, patiently waiting for someone to enter into his kingdom so he could do just that. They showed love with food, and there was no shortage of either.

My grandparents taught me what it meant to have nothing but to give everything. They were the ones who gave me some of my very first lessons on empathy and kindness. They had little to nothing themselves, but they gave to those in need whenever they could because they knew how it felt to walk in those same worn-out shoes.

Grandpa wasn't perfect by any means—he had a quick temper, held onto grudges for years, and probably held a few regrets, I'm sure. But he did two things perfectly—he believed in being a good human first, and he loved his people with all his heart.

When he died, he was at home, surrounded by the ones he loved. All forty-some of *his people* sat around his bedside and held his hand as he left this world. He lived a good, long life and died an even better death.

That's how I want to leave this earth, inspiring warm memories, leaving love, and spreading kindness long after I entered my grave. And how I wanted to die started now, with how I intended to live.

One day, I'll only be a memory for someone. I'm going to do my best to be a good one.

Something that piqued my interest when I Googled *what to do before you die* was the regret of not attending certain concerts live due to the outrageous cost of tickets. I was stuck on that bullet point for a long time, because I, myself, never booked or attended concerts for the same reason. I didn't want to have the same regret later on, and took the search results to heart.

As it happened, Elton John would soon be coming through Saskatoon on his farewell tour, but, needless to say, the tickets were pricey. In the middle of the night, from beneath my bed-sheets where all of my secret online shopping is done without Mikey knowing, I typed in my credit card digits and pressed enter. I booked Elton's concert a year in advance because I wanted to go, and the cost didn't matter. *I mean, how many retirement concerts could Elton John possibly have left?* I knew this was a once-in-a-lifetime opportunity.

The name of the tour was "Farewell Yellow Brick Road."[23]

My healing journey really was like the Yellow Brick Road in *The Wonderful World of Oz*, winding and twisting through my lessons and adventures. As I walked that road, some new friends joined me. I gained the courage to be my authentic self. I gained the wisdom to let go of the control I had once so desperately craved. I took things less seriously and learned to love myself. I learned to belong and began to live a life led by faith and heart.

---

23 I know, I can't make this stuff up!

That's when the real magic happened—it's when my life really started to take off.

My coming-home moment happened when I attended a meeting my workplace holds each summer. It was the meeting I had dreamed of attending for nearly a decade, what I saw as the "crème de la crème of meetings" at my workplace. In my eyes, an invitation to attend was like winning the golden ticket. I had worked the entire length of my career just to be invited to it and, even after establishing my new work boundaries, I finally got that invitation.

The invitation confirmed that I had made the right choice to leave my work ambitions behind for now. Even after I had stepped aside from the corporate ladder, I somehow still made it to the meeting I had always aspired to be at. My choice to be a mother first and an employee second never felt so good.

Still, I was a bundle of nerves for days before I left for the trip. I hadn't shopped for business formal in nearly four years, let alone interacted with only colleagues for three days in a row in all that time. A quick shopping trip later, I had remedied at least one of those problems and felt almost ready to face the other.

As my plane descended into the city the night before the big meeting, the butterflies in my stomach started having a dance party of their own. The next morning, I tried on three different outfits before I felt satisfied. As I applied my makeup, I almost missed the fact that Weston wasn't there to rear-end me while I put on my mascara. I'm mean, where was the action? I sipped hot coffee while I worked on perfecting my eyeliner, hoping it would soothe my frazzled nerves.

I stopped to take a full, deep breath. *You're finally here. Don't let your nerves get the better of you now.*

Gazing into the mirror, I thought of what my mother would say to me in this instance.

"Own it, Sharbear. Regardless of how long it took you to get here or the winding road of unexpected turns life took you on, you are here. Stop being so nervous. Someone wanted you here, so be present and own it."

She had always taught me to be present, especially when you arrive. When I left my hotel room for the day-long meeting, I had my mother's confidence tucked in my back pocket.

To my complete surprise, the meeting was dreadfully boring. A blur of PowerPoint slides flew across the stage screen for hours with no end in sight. As my attention wandered, I found myself wanting to be at home playing with the boys or hastily preparing chicken nuggets before running the boys to their next sporting activity. I nearly laughed out loud at the irony.

I'd wanted to sit at this conference table for years, and now, I could barely keep my attention on what was happening. You see, I could still *play* the part—carrying the perfect, black briefcase and wearing the business-approved heels—but I no longer required myself to *be* the part. Still, a sense of pride and self-recognition came over me for making it to the table I was sitting at—that moment was ten years in the making. I sat in the presence of my accomplishments and appreciated everything motherhood had taught me.

I reflected on who I had become and what I had created. I had created an opportunity to have a career that allowed me to contribute to my family financially and be a good mother at the same time. My decision helped my family thrive as a unit and left my marriage in one piece.

Attending this meeting was so much more than attending *just* another meeting. It was confirmation of the growth I had experienced over the last five years. Sitting at the table, I owned *all* of my job descriptions—mother, employee, bookkeeper, wife. I wore my hats proudly—even my clown nose.

Stepping back in my career wasn't easy, but it was a compromise that permitted my soul to take the direction it needed to go. Shedding the ego mask from my true self also allowed my family to join me on the ride. As lost as I was during those initial baby years when I first returned to work, it had all been worth it—because in the end, I had found myself.

The first thing I did upon my arrival at home was run a steaming, hot bath to decompress. I was overjoyed to be back in my pyjamas and in our comfortable home. As I applied my nightly skin regime before heading to bed, I stopped and looked at the woman staring back at me from the mirror and smiled. I quite liked what I saw.

Five short years ago, I had to force myself to lock eyes with that same reflection while I said positive affirmations. Not anymore. Now, I couldn't stop gazing at the beautiful, glowing reflection. I could no longer claim the freshness and effortless beauty of youth, but I had something better—witchy wrinkles, grey hair, and laugh lines from cackling too much. Everything about me was totally fabulous.

Owning my flaws made me feel immaculate and unblemished within. Instead of feeling resentment and self-loathing, I now saw my reflection in the mirror with empathy, tenderness, and kindness. I was beautiful inside, and only because motherhood had put me on another path.

I was whole.

On my quest, I'd learned that what we want isn't always what we need. The universe, God, a mighty man called Oz—whoever is out there—had found a way for me to attend that coveted meeting when the time was right, not when *I* thought it was right. When I let go of the need to control every aspect of my life, intuition and trust took over. Unexpected life experiences showed me how to lead with my heart and not my head.

A few months after that Golden Ticket meeting, I sat in a concert hall and watched one of the legends of modern pop give the performance of a lifetime and speak about his own yellow brick road journey. The iconic Elton John had forged his own path against all odds to live the life he chose. Despite not knowing him on a personal basis, I couldn't help but resonate with his story of resilience.

I sat in complete awe when he began to play his live rendition of "Tiny Dancer". In an instant, I was back in the moment two years earlier when, yearning for a small taste of happiness, I had downloaded that exact song to begin my first playlist. Here I was now, listening to the song live, happy, whole, and present. I was living my life out in real time. Looking back, I could see that the winding route I had taken had been as rich as my arrival.

The thing of it is, if you walk far enough, you'll eventually come to some place—that's how walking works. I simply had to start walking in the right direction to get to my next place, even if I didn't know exactly where that *next* place was. And when I arrived, gosh darn it, I discovered I'd always been wearing the enchanted heels that would take me home. The magic to heal was in me all along.

And the same magic is in *you*.

You have the power to heal yourself, right now. You have all of the tools you need at your fingertips. You have the power to bring light, love, and gratitude into your life, each and every magical day you get to wake up. Remember, living a better life starts with you— so live on purpose, and not just because. Time spent being present is never time wasted, it's a life well-lived.

I truly believe every experience in your life is meant for you—nothing is by accident. The hard lessons—the ones you'd rather not experience—are the ones that actually move you further along your winding road. So learn to trust each one when it comes, even if it comes in the form of a flying house. And most importantly, listen to the voice in your heart—that'll be your ultimate guide home.

Now, go get 'em—I've taught you everything you need to know. May you find wisdom, courage, and love along your own journey. Once you do, you might just become the envy of everyone along the Yellow Brick Road. And if you ever feel lost, know I'll be ten bricks behind you, cheering you on every step of the way.

Love,
S.

Acknowledgments

Bentley and Weston, thank you for letting Mommy feverishly write, edit, and publish the story you gave me. God knew what I needed when he made me your mother. You changed my life for the better—because you exist, I am fully alive and present. I will be forever grateful for both of you.

Mike, thank you for allowing me to share some of our stories to a broader audience. Thank you for accepting me, as is. You loved me even when I didn't like my own skin suit. From the bottom of my heart, I know I could never find another you.

Talena, you possess a true gift, my friend. The fairy-tale twist of the story appeared only when you decided to join me on the ride—revision is truly where the magic happens. As a novice, I thank you for your guidance, expertise, and diligence throughout this evolving and everlasting project. You pushed me when I didn't think I could go on and made me believe in myself. People become who they are by emulating the likeness of who they want to be. I can only hope to one day be as captivating of a writer as you.

Jennifer, Shirley, and Laura, thank you for allowing me to share some of our stories together, too. All three of you have shaped my story in some way, shape, or form. When I'm interviewed on my favourite daytime television show, I'll be sure to mention all of you and your influences in my life.

Pamela, thank you for always being one phone call or text message away. During the writing, editing, and publishing of this book, I often reached my limit, and felt like throwing in the towel for good. That's when I knew to call you. From ensuring I hired a professional editor, used the proper comma, or understood the basics behind copyright laws, you were there whenever I needed solid advice. (The *Hang in There Kitty* meme was my favourite.) Readers are holding this book because of you.

Next, much love and thanks to my incredibly supportive network of readers, especially if you were with me from my initial blogging days. Sharing some of my secrets in blog form sometimes left me gasping for air. But I pressed enter anyway. I was immensely comforted when readers like you reached out and thanked me for my honesty, truth, and vulnerability.

Lastly, and in no particular order, I'd like to give a big shout out to my literary heroes in the world—Elizabeth Gilbert, Cheryl Strayed, Brené Brown, Gary Zukav, Gabby Bernstein, Rachel Hollis, Glennon Doyle, Elizabeth Lesser, Amanda Lindhout, Shauna Niequist, and Jeannette Walls. Each of your creative masterpieces describing resilience, bravery, and vulnerability helped to make me whole again. On more than one occasion, your experiences, wisdom, and advice furthered me along on my healing journey. Thank you for sharing your stories. I wouldn't be the person I am today without you.

About the Author

SHARI CHELACK is a boss babe by day and mommy extraordinaire by night, married to her one and only, Mikey. In her daily juggling act, she considers her most important job title to be the mother of two dashing young boys, Bentley and Weston. She's both a nature nut and a silver linings addict, hanging her coat up in the heart of Saskatchewan, Canada. As an avid bookworm and wanderer, she has found both vices to have seriously damaged her ignorance along the way. *Flawed & Fabulous* is her latest adventure and her first published book.

References

Baum, L. Frank. *The Wonderful Wizard of Oz.* Chicago: George M. Hill Company, 1900.

Brown, Brené. *Rising Strong: How the Ability to Reset Transforms the Way We Live, Love, Parent, and Lead.* New York: Random House, 2015.

"Emerald City," Wikimedia Foundation, last modified May 30, 2020, 22:45, https://en.wikipedia.org/wiki/Emerald_City

"Gillian Lynne," Wikimedia Foundation, last modified May 18, 2020, 18:51, https://en.wikipedia.org/wiki/Gillian_Lynne.

Hollis, Rachel. *Girl, Wash Your Face: Stop Believing the Lies About Who You Are So You Can Become Who You Were Meant to Be.* Nashville: Thomas Nelson, 2018.

"Kintsugi," Wikimedia Foundation, last modified June 28, 2020, 07:51, https://en.wikipedia.org/wiki/Kintsugi.

Lesser, Elizabeth. *Marrow: A Love Story.* New York: HarperCollins Publishers, 2016.

Llenas, Anna. *The Color Monster: A Pop-Up Book of Feelings.* New York: Sterling Publishing Co., Inc., 2015.

Niequist, Shauna. *Present Over Perfect: Leaving Behind Frantic for a Simpler, More Soulful Way of Living.* Grand Rapids: Zondervan, 2016.

"Rat Park," Wikimedia Foundation, last modified June 21, 2020, 14:49, https://en.wikipedia.org/wiki/Rat_Park.

Robinson, Sir Ken. *Do Schools Kill Creativity?* TED, February 2006. Accessed April 5, 2020. https://www.ted.com/talks/sir_ken_robinson_do_schools_kill_creativity.

Strayed, Cheryl. *Wild: From Lost to Found on the Pacific Crest Trail.* New York: Random House, 2012.

Zukav, Gary. *The Seat of the Soul.* New York: Simon & Schuster Paperbacks, 1989.

Endnotes

*   Baum, *The Wonderful Wizard of Oz*, 27.

†   "Kintsugi," Wikimedia.

‡   Hollis, *Girl, Wash Your Face*, 31.

§   "Emerald City," Wikimedia.

¶   Zukav, *The Seat of the Soul*, 131.

**   "Rat Park," Wikimedia.

††   Llenas, *The Color Monster*, 5.

‡‡   Brown, *Rising Strong*, 50.

§§   Robinson, "Do Schools Kill Creativity?"

¶¶   "Gillian Lynne," Wikimedia.

***   Niequist, *Present Over Perfect*, 55.

††† Strayed, *Wild*, 51.

‡‡‡ Lesser, *Marrow*, 3.

Made in the USA
Middletown, DE
29 October 2020

22884990R00116